CLEAN & DELICIOUS

with Dani Spies

CLEAN & DELICIOUS

with *Dani Spies*

eat clean and get healthy
with 100 whole-ingredient recipes

DK

Publisher Mike Sanders
Art Director William Thomas
Senior Editors Molly Ahuja and Brook Farling
Designer Lindsay Dobbs
Photographers Rikki Snyder, Helene McGuire, and Daniel Showalter
Food Stylists Leslie Orlandini and Lovoni Walker
Proofreader Claire Safran
Indexer Johnna VanHoose Dinse

First American Edition, 2023
Published in the United States by DK Publishing
1745 Broadway, 20th Floor, New York, NY 10019

The authorized representative in the EEA is
Dorling Kindersley Verlag GmbH.
Arnulfstr. 124, 80636 Munich, Germany

Copyright © 2023 Dorling Kindersley Limited
DK, a Division of Penguin Random House LLC
23 24 25 26 27 10 9 8 7 6 5 4 3 2 1
001– 334473– APR/2023

A catalog record for this book
is available from the Library of Congress.
ISBN 978-0-7440-7700-1

DK books are available at special discounts when purchased in bulk for sales promotions, premiums, fund-raising, or educational use. For details, contact: DK Publishing Special Markets,
1745 Broadway, 20th Floor, New York, NY 10019
SpecialSales@dk.com

Printed and bound in Canada

For the curious
www.dk.com

MIX
Paper | Supporting
responsible forestry
FSC™ C018179

This book was made with Forest Stewardship Council ™ certified paper - one small step in DK's commitment to a sustainable future. **For more information go to www.dk.com/our-green-pledge**

ABOUT THE AUTHOR

DANI SPIES is a mom, food blogger, holistic weight loss coach, Holistic Health Counselor (HHC), and the founder of the Clean & Delicious website and Clean & Delicious YouTube channel where she teaches her followers how to cook and eat clean in order to get healthy and lose weight. In addition to her practical, easy approach to healthy cooking and eating, Dani coaches her followers on the mental and emotional aspects of healthy eating and cooking so they can reach their personal wellness and weight loss goals without constantly being on the diet rollercoaster. Her mission is to help her followers eat better, cook more, and relax as they follow their paths to health, wellness, and weight loss, without the need to count calories or obsess over every meal.

CONTENTS

1 Introduction

WELCOME

Welcome! If we haven't met, I'm Dani Spies—I'm a mom, food blogger, YouTuber, and health, wellness, and weight loss coach (among many other things!). I often joke that I am a foodie first, health nut second.

I love eating, cooking, and enjoying real, whole, healthy foods but never at the expense of flavor. I believe that food is one of life's true pleasures and I know that if anyone wants to eat better, feel better, and reach their personal health and weight goals—their food has to taste great! If your food isn't delicious, you won't want to eat it, which will make your attempts at healthy eating fruitless. Simply put, eating tasteless food in the name of health is not enjoyable and therefore not sustainable.

Believe me, I know! I began dieting in the fifth grade and continued jumping on and off diets for nearly 15 years. Raise your hand if you remember Slim Fast? A shake for breakfast, a shake for lunch, and a reasonable dinner. That was just one of many insane diet plans I tried to adhere to throughout the years.

At the time, I believed sacrificing flavor and restricting food was the path to health, wellness, and happiness. But trying to control and restrict my food never actually helped me to lose weight or feel any healthier. Instead, it led to years of yo-yo dieting, binge eating late at night, and sneaking food when no one was looking.

For years I thought I was a willpower weakling and had no self control. But I now know that neither of those were true. Our bodies are simply not designed to be deprived of pleasure. If you want to have a healthy relationship with food, it starts with the love of food.

It's my intention to help you prepare and eat foods that not only taste great, but that make you feel great as well. I've picked up lots of tips and tricks along my journey of learning to eat well and I plan to share them all with you. I promise delicious and nutritious food can easily coexist and I'm going to do my best to make this feel super doable.

XO,
Dani

GROWING UP

I grew up in a small cape-style house in northern New Jersey with one sister (Kristi) who was 15 months older than me. While our household wasn't 100% Italian (my mom is Irish and German and my dad is Italian), the majority of the meals we ate were classic American-Italian dishes.

Both my mom and dad enjoyed cooking and were really good at it.

I remember my mom spending hours each weekend making meals for the busy week to come. Some of my childhood staples included escarole and beans (page 167), stuffed peppers (page 216), lasagna, baked chicken with potatoes and onions, pasta fagioli, broccoli rabe and garlic (page 153), and beef barley soup.

And let me tell you, there was nothing better than the smell of her homemade meat sauce simmering on the stove every Sunday for us to enjoy over a plate of macaroni on busy weeknights.

My parents were meal-prepping well before meal prep was a thing and we ate together pretty much every night of the week. Food was fun, delicious, and nourishing, and whether we had something to talk about or were quietly eating around the table, food brought us together.

***In our home, food was love ...
until I began dieting in the 5th grade.***

DIETING

It's crazy to think that I was just 10 years old when I tried my first diet, but I did. The irony is that I wasn't overweight, but my young brain picked up the message that dieting would make me skinny, beautiful, and forever happy. Plus, dieting seemed like the norm to me—I had friends who were dieting, my mom was a dieter, just about everyone on TV seemed to be dieting, and I even remember one of my favorite teachers talking about the new diet she was on.

In my mind, being on a diet made me healthy (and cool), but in reality, dieting led me to years of having a very unhealthy relationship with food as I struggled with my weight and body.

STUDIES

This struggle eventually led me away from my desire to go to culinary school and brought me straight to studying fitness, nutrition, and the role that our emotional and mental wellness play in our relationship with food and body.

I received my certification as a Holistic Health Counselor (HHC) after graduating from The Institute of Integrative Nutrition in New York City. I've studied with Marc David at The Institute for The Psychology of Eating and completed the professional cooking series at The New School of Cooking in Culver City. I'm a weight loss coach under Master Coach,

Brooke Castillo of The Life Coach School and I hold a B.A. in Psychology from William Paterson University.

The combination of these studies paired with a lifetime of experience taught me how to shift out of my diet mentality into a place of health, nourishment, pleasure, and connection. Which of course, brought me back to my original love—food and cooking!

By making small, consistent changes in my approach to health and weight loss, I was able to drop my struggle with food and body, lose the 25 pounds I was constantly battling with, reclaim my natural love of food and cooking, AND I've been able to maintain those changes for over 15 years.

MY INTENTION

I'm on a mission to help you eat better, cook more, and relax into the journey of health, wellness, and weight loss without the insanity of traditional dieting.

My intention in the kitchen is to make healthy eating crazy easy and insanely delicious. I want to help you cut through all of the nutritional drama and give you permission to relax around the whole "healthy eating" thing so you can enjoy simple, delicious, nutritious foods that will naturally support your health and wellness goals.

I appreciate you being here!

WHY WE OVEREAT
It's Not Due to Lack of Willpower

When I was in the throes of my weight struggles, overeating was my biggest challenge, as is the case for most people in a similar state. We have a desire to eat even when not hungry and/or we have strong cravings for foods that don't align with our health and weight goals.

For many years, when trying to solve the weight loss puzzle, I believed I simply needed to strengthen my willpower and self-discipline. I put ALL of my attention and energy into trying to control the food I was eating. I was always trying new dietary approaches and thinking there was some type of food plan that would help me end my overeating struggles once and for all.

But what I eventually realized is that while food is VERY important, it's really just one spoke on the wheel of health, wellness, and weight loss. To understand our habits with food and overeating, we often have to zoom out to look beyond food and adopt a broader perspective.

I have found there are five main causes of overeating, and you may be surprised to know that only one of them has to do with food.

1. EATING ACCORDING TO A PLAN

When we get into the habit of following diets or trying to eat in accordance with a dietary plan or system, we become dependent on external sources of information to dictate when and how much we should be eating. We often make decisions about what and when to eat based on the latest diet fad, the clock, or by what our friends are eating. We also tend to make these choices based upon what we think rather than as a response to the natural hunger cues we receive from our bodies. An easy tool you can use to help rebuild the trust between you and your body is to simply pause before eating and ask yourself, "Am I hungry?" Close your eyes and turn inward, scanning your body for feedback. Trust what you sense. If you don't detect any natural hunger signals, wait for 30-60 minutes and check in again.

2. QUALITY FOOD

The quality of the food we eat is one of the most important factors in determining if we will feel satiated and satisfied after a meal. When we eat, our bodies are looking to be energized and nourished by the foods we choose, so if the base of your diet consists of low-quality, highly processed foods that are void of nutrients and lack in fiber, protein, and healthy fats, you'll find yourself feeling hungry after a meal. Remember, your body is not only looking for calories when you eat, it's also looking for vitamins, minerals, and nutrients. This is why I love the practice of focusing on real, whole, foods as close to their natural state as possible, most of the time. It's an easy way to point yourself in the direction of eating higher quality foods without following an excess of unnecessary food rules.

3. ATTENTION & AWARENESS

As we all live in a very busy world that moves at a very quick pace, we tend to mimic this pace when we eat. We eat quickly, on the go, as an afterthought, and without our attention. Have you ever found yourself standing at the counter while you eat, eating straight from the fridge, eating in your car, or eating on the couch while watching TV? It's very common to eat without paying attention to the taste, textures, and aroma of the food. We can't forget that food is meant to be pleasurable and the pleasure that food provides via taste, texture, and aroma, plays a big role in the nourishment and satisfaction we receive from a meal.

4. EATING OVER EMOTIONS

Emotional eating is a big topic and one I could write an entire book about. But for the sake of this chapter, I will keep it simple. It's important to create an awareness around when you choose to eat to solve for your emotions and when you choose to eat to solve for biological hunger. If you find yourself reaching for food when you are not hungry, to help ease or distract you from uncomfortable or unwanted emotions—simply take note. Do not use this as a reason to beat yourself up. You are not broken or a willpower weakling. You are simply trying your best, in the moment, to care for yourself. We turn to food to ease emotions for one good reason—it works, albeit extremely temporarily. The practice of learning to allow and process emotions is work worth doing, but realize it has absolutely nothing to do with food. If emotional eating is an obstacle for you, remind yourself that trying to control or restrict your food is not the solution. Our emotions are like little messengers that can help us better understand ourselves and our true desires. Practice being more mindful of your emotions, so you can better understand what they are wanting to communicate with you.

5. REST

Our bodies are truly brilliant and always working to maintain homeostasis, which is simply another way of saying that our bodies work to stay in balance. When we are tired and try to push through, our bodies will create cravings for processed foods, specifically flour and sugar (think chips, crackers, candies, and pastries). It does this for good reason as the body knows that these highly processed foods will offer us the quickest boost of energy (it takes very little effort to break these foods down since they are so highly processed). Have you ever noticed that you have strong cravings when you feel fatigued or that it's just harder to avoid foods that you wouldn't normally eat when you feel tired? Now you know why! The next time you find yourself feeling sleepy, don't try wrestling with your food cravings. Instead, make a plan to be sure you get some more sleep that night or sneak in a cat nap when possible.

I share this to remind you that food is simply one part of our health, wellness, and weight loss journey. Food is not the enemy, it is a beautiful, delicious, pleasurable part of our life that both nourishes our bodies and keeps us alive! Having a healthy relationship with food is rooted in loving and celebrating the food you eat (not trying to control and restrict it), and it is my intention to help fuel and honor that relationship with the recipes and tips throughout this book.

WHY DIETS DON'T WORK:
The Diet Mentality

Each year, more than 50% of American adults try to lose weight, yet research shows that diets rarely work. As a matter of fact, 90–97% of people who lose weight through dieting will gain back the weight, likely within 2–5 years.

I'm very familiar with this cycle, as I spent a good 15 years of my life jumping on and off of different diet plans, constantly losing and gaining the same 25 pounds. I was in constant search of the perfect diet, believing that somehow the answers and information that I so desperately wanted could be gleaned from the next book, diet plan, or nutritional expert.

I was hyper focused on food, often restricting major food groups, skipping meals, and trying to control what I ate. In this desperate attempt to change my body, I wasn't taking care of myself. I never considered how I felt, what I was thinking, nor did I pay attention to the feedback my body provided. I really believed that if I could just stick to the plan, I would reach my goals and never have to struggle with food or my weight again. You may not be surprised to know that this approach never worked for me, at least not in a sustainable way.

I was stuck in a diet mentality.

WHAT IS A DIET MENTALITY?

A diet mentality is when we believe there is a perfect way of eating that will help us reach our goals if we can just find and follow the perfect plan. It's a false notion that the external information we get from a dietary plan is more valuable than the internal needs and feedback that we get from our bodies, lifestyle, and instincts.

Outside sources can provide great information, great guidelines, and amazing resources for us. They can be very useful tools along our journey. But when we push and bully ourselves to stick to a plan, leaning on willpower to white knuckle our way to the finish line, we are in a diet mentality. This approach to health and weight loss rarely fuels our ability to create sustainable change.

When we hand all of our power over to the external plan and never take the time to consider our internal experience on this plan, we are in a diet mentality. With a diet mentality we never actually include ourselves on the journey. We are not paying attention to the feedback from our bodies or our experience. A diet mentality is when we put all of the power into the plan and we don't take any personal responsibility to find the path that works best for ourselves.

THE "PERFECT" DIET

Here's something that might surprise you—there is no one diet (or food!) in and of itself that is good, bad, right, wrong, better or worse. All diets are meant to be used as a guideline, not as a strict set of rules. Different things work for different people. That's why there are so many different dietary approaches out there. No dietary approach will ever work for you sustainably if you try to approach it without your own individual feedback.

As my mentor often says, many of us are on a "high-fact diet," meaning that we are so overwhelmed with intellectual information about what we should and shouldn't eat that we lose touch with the wisest expert we have access to: ourselves and our bodies.

THE SHIFT

It wasn't until I became pregnant with my daughter, who is now 13 years old, that I was able to shift out of the diet mentality. I didn't completely understand it at the time, but I now know that being pregnant was the first time in my adult life I actually gave myself permission to be in the body I was in. Instead of trying to change my body, I wanted to learn how to take really good care of my body.

Instead of trying to force myself to stick to a bunch of external rules, I used the external information as a gentle guideline and spent more time being curious about and getting to know my internal experience with food and my body.

POWERFUL QUESTIONS

Whether you are experimenting with my Clean & Delicious basic eating guidelines or another eating approach that resonates with you, here are some powerful questions to ask yourself when trying to create healthier eating habits that will support your health and weight loss goals.

Grab a pen and a notebook and explore:

- *Does this work for me?*
- *What exactly about this is working for me?*
- *What exactly about this is not working for me?*
- *What would make this feel better for me?*
- *What would make this feel easier for me?*
- *How can I adjust this in a way that would support my personal preferences and lifestyle?*
- *Is there another way that I can think about this?*
- *Can I reframe this in a way that would serve me better?*

Remember: there is no perfect diet and our approach to eating is likely to change throughout our lifetime. We are in a constant relationship with food and our bodies and so it's an ongoing practice that looks like this: observe, learn, tweak, adjust, repeat.

THERE IS NO WAGON

When we are in a diet mentality, we are either on or off the wagon with our healthy eating habits (if you have ever been on a diet, I trust you know exactly what I mean). But shifting out of the diet mentality means letting go of the wagon. There is no getting on the wagon and getting off of the wagon, because there's simply no wagon. Healthy eating habits are a continuum.

Every choice either works for us or gives us an opportunity to learn more about ourselves. Everything moves you forward when there's no wagon. Instead of a wagon, we are making an ongoing commitment to figuring out what works for our bodies and our lifestyles no matter how long it takes or how many slip-ups we have.

Everything we learn is information that we can use to help move us toward our goals as long as we are not slipping into an all-or-nothing, perfectionist way of thinking. I believe that all things move us forward as long as we stay committed to ourselves.

I encourage you to stay open and stay curious. Remember that you are as important as the approach you use and you cannot do this without yourself or in spite of yourself.

Anytime you notice your diet mentality trying to sneak in and convince you that a linear road of perfection is the path to sustainable health or weight loss, I would like you to simply smile and remind yourself that eating well and working on weight goals is a practice and a journey, not a destination.

A BEGINNER'S GUIDE TO HEALTHY EATING
15 Clean & Delicious Tips

Whether you are new to healthy eating or simply want to work more healthy eating habits into your lifestyle, looking toward small changes that you can commit to and practice over a long period of time is where the magic lives.

We often think that in order to create the healthy changes we desire, we have to do a big overhaul with our eating habits, so we try to change everything all at once. We tend to take on too much too fast and then wonder why we are unable to sustain the changes for longer than a week or so.

Creating a lifestyle shift is not something you do overnight—it's not about jumping on another fad diet or following the newest health craze. Rather, it's a day-to-day practice of shifting your thoughts, beliefs and habits to align with the goals you desire.

This journey has to be rooted in self-love, self-kindness and self-compassion. It's a practice; which brings me to my very first tip:

1. ALLOW YOURSELF TO BE ON THE JOURNEY.

When you are a beginner, adapting to new habits and creating lifestyle changes is a practice and will take some time. You are learning how to do new things and just like a child learning how to walk, you have to give yourself grace, space and time to figure it out. You're not supposed to know every step all at once, nor do you have to change everything all in the first week. You don't have to have all of your food perfectly meal-prepped and you don't have to give up all your favorite foods. I want you to notice what you feel ready for—ask yourself, "What feels doable? What do I feel ready to commit to?" If you notice your brain wanting to jump into all-or-nothing type of thinking, recognize that this is a diet mentality and it never works. Give yourself permission to slow down and create some space to experiment and learn.

2. HEALTHY EATING IS NOT THE SAME FOR EVERYONE.

There are so many different approaches to eating well that work. As much as I wish I could tell you the one perfect way to eat that works for everyone, I can't, because it doesn't exist. You can eat well and be a vegan or a vegetarian. You can eat well and be a meat-eater, a weightlifter, or a yogi. You can eat well and enjoy two meals a day and you can eat well and enjoy six meals a day. My point is, it varies. Different things work for different people at different points in their life. There are no hard and fast rules when it comes to healthy eating outside of my base Clean & Delicious philosophy. Simply focus on real, whole, unprocessed foods as close to their natural state as possible most of the time and that whatever you choose to eat, you do it with awareness so you can really enjoy it.

3. COOK AS OFTEN AS YOU CAN.

Cooking is one of the easiest ways to start eating better because you are in charge. And here's the deal: that doesn't mean you have to cook every single thing you eat, you just want to get into the practice of cooking more often than not.

4. FOCUS ON QUALITY OVER CALORIES.

I have found that for many people, definitely for myself, focusing on calories tends to leave you feeling deprived and restricted. This is because when we focus on calories, we tend to be focused on what we "shouldn't" be eating, what we need to avoid or reduce and what we need to eliminate—this is a a scarcity mentality. But when you shift that focus to quality, your brain starts looking for all of the delicious, beautiful foods that it gets to add into the diet. You begin to notice the abundance of options that are available to you and from this space, food becomes delightful, fun and creative again! Not only does this feel good, but you'll begin to notice how healthy foods taste good as well.

5. WHAT GROWS TOGETHER, GOES TOGETHER.

Foods that grow in the same season automatically taste great together because Mother Nature always has our back. And this is great to know because it takes a lot of guesswork out of cooking. You can simply trust the seasons to lead the way. Combinations like berries, tomatoes and basil, Brussels sprouts and grapes, or butternut squash and cranberries are all great examples of ingredients that are grown in the same season and pair really well together. Be open to picking up a new seasonal ingredient when you are at the grocery store. One way to do this is to experiment with buying one 'new-to-you' ingredient each week and have some fun exploring, cooking and tasting new foods. When you buy foods that are in season, they have the best flavor while offering the most nutritional value, so it really is a win-win.

6. BACK-POCKET RECIPES.

When transitioning into healthier eating you want to create some back-pocket recipes for yourself, meaning recipes that you know you enjoy and can make in a reasonable amount of time. These recipes should be complete no-brainers, so you can lean on them when you don't have the time or desire to plan and think ahead. You want to have a couple "BPRs" for breakfast, lunch and dinner. And then you can slowly add to your arsenal by experimenting with new recipes and putting the keepers in your back pocket. A few of my go-to, back pocket recipes include: Hard-Boiled Eggs (page 53), my Go-to Green Smoothie (page 63), Rotisserie Chicken Salad (page 124), and Easy Chicken and Broccoli Quesadillas (page 230). These are all meals I can make with my eyes closed that I enjoy and help me stay aligned with goals.

7. LEARN TO READ YOUR LABELS.

Learning to read the labels on your food is a great way to get a sense of what is going into your body. To keep things easy and aligned with eating real, whole foods, focus on the ingredients. A good general rule of thumb is to stick to foods that have five ingredients or less, and to make sure you can recognize and pronounce each of those ingredients.

8. AVOID HIGHLY PROCESSED FOODS.

Let me begin by saying that a lot of healthy foods are slightly processed. Oatmeal is slightly processed, quinoa is slightly processed, frozen veggies are slightly processed. If your food is not coming straight from the field or the farm, it's going to have gone through a series of processing. But these are not the types of processed foods I am referring to and certainly not the foods you want to avoid. Rather, I want you to be on the lookout for foods that go through many phases of processing before they actually make it to your plate. These are foods that are made in factories and are sometimes called "Frankenfoods." Remember, you want your body to do the work of breaking down and processing the foods that you eat, so the more a food is processed outside of your body, the less nutritional value it's going to offer.

The ingredient list is a great indicator of how processed a food is; when foods have long ingredient lists, chances are they are highly processed. Other than being nutritionally void, highly processed foods are often high in low-quality sugars, fats and salts. When we get an overload of fat, sugar, and salt we can no longer appreciate the delicious subtleties of real natural whole foods and I do believe that this is why healthy eating often gets a bad rap. If you are used to eating highly processed foods and your taste buds have adjusted to unnatural, high processed flavors, you will not be able to taste and appreciate the flavor of real whole foods.

9. AVOID ARTIFICIAL FLAVORS AND SWEETENERS AS OFTEN AS POSSIBLE.

Artificial flavors and sweeteners are not real foods, they are food-like products that are made in factories and designed to bypass the logical part of your brain while triggering all of your pleasure points. This often creates cravings for more sweet and artificially flavored foods that do not align with your healthy eating intentions.

Some also find that these types of foods can lead to overeating as they trigger beliefs "that we can have an unlimited amount of them, since they don't really count anyway" (if you've ever been on a diet, I trust you know what I am talking about).

10. PRACTICE MEAL PREPPING.

Meal prepping doesn't mean that you have to have all of your meals perfectly prepared and measured out ahead of time nor does it mean you have to have an Instagram-worthy stocked fridge. But taking small steps to have some food prepared ahead of time can solve half the battle for many of us who are trying to eat better. Cooking ahead and making enough so that you can enjoy those meals two or three times throughout the week can be such a huge help when you are trying to eat better. Start small by making a big pot of soup to have on hand for the week, or make some overnight oats so your breakfast is ready to go.

11. STOCK YOUR PANTRY AND FREEZER.

Having some healthy staples in your pantry and freezer is a huge help when you need to keep things super simple. I love having canned beans, olives, salmon, tuna, and canned soups on hand in my pantry and foods like frozen fruits and veggies, veggie burgers, and frozen brown rice or quinoa, for times when I need to keep things quick and easy. See my Fridge, Freezer, and Pantry Staples on pages 35 and 38.

HONOR YOUR HUNGER.

So many of us are in the habit of relying on our minds (instead of our bodies) to decide when to eat. We eat according to the clock, a diet, or by what all of 'the experts' tell us that we lose touch with our built-in biological hunger signals. Reconnecting with your natural hunger cues is a practice and is your best bet for effortless long-term healthy eating because you don't have to think about food so much, you just feel it. A good practice when you are reconnecting natural hunger cues is to close your eyes, put your hand on your belly and ask your body if it needs fuel. Look for subtle signs like lower energy, lack of focus, shakiness, a belly growl, or constant thoughts about food. Again, it's a practice, so give yourself the space and the time to relearn how to connect to your huge cues.

12. KNOW YOUR "WHY".

So often we try to create change from a place of, 'I need to, I have to, or I really should', but realize that all of these thoughts create negative motivation which rarely works in a sustainable way. I encourage you to think about why you want to eat better. What are the positive reasons for wanting to have a healthy relationship with your food, body and self? Perhaps you want to feel lighter, feel better, or have more energy to live the life you want to live. Connecting to why this change feels important to you as your "why" will become your anchor as you navigate new habits and lifestyle changes. Take the time to identify your "why", write it down and then read it in the morning and in the evening so you can keep your mind aligned in the direction you are moving towards.

13. HEALTH EXTENDS BEYOND THE FOOD WE EAT.

When it comes to healthy eating, what we eat is important but it's not all that matters. How you eat, where you eat, when you eat and who you are eating with also play a role in your health. For instance, if you are in a hurry, eating a plate of organic steamed chicken and broccoli that you don't particularly enjoy is actually a very unhealthy eating experience. While you may be avoiding toxins from your food, you are still creating them in your body as a result of your toxic thinking. On the flip-side, imagine you are with your family or a dear friend, sitting down to one of your favorite childhood meals made from scratch. The meal was made with love, you are being nourished by the people and the environment you are in, and so regardless of the food on your plate, this is a very healthy and nourishing eating experience. So pay attention to the choices you make and why. Pay attention to the stories you are telling yourself and the food you eat. And of course, as often as possible, try to eat in an environment and with other people that feed and nourish you as well.

14. BE EASY.

Contrary to popular belief, there is no rush and there is no finish line, so be easy with yourself and give yourself permission to practice the healthy eating habits that you want to embody. There is no perfect way of eating as different things work for different people. My recommendation is this: experiment, observe, tweak, and repeat. Don't get fanatic about things, simply allow yourself to practice and learn.

NUTRITION SIMPLIFIED

There's a lot of information in the world about nutrition and so many different opinions on what we all should and should not be eating. And while many of these opinions directly contradict one another, they all seem to have scientific-based evidence to prove them true. It's no wonder so many people feel confused and overwhelmed about what to eat. With an excess of nutritional noise, we tend to forget the simple food truths that we know to be true on some level.

This is why I like to keep food easy without an abundance of unnecessary rules.

I'm simply here to remind you of what you already know when it comes to eating well—focus on eating real, whole, unprocessed foods, as close to their natural state as possible, most of the time.

Whatever foods you choose to eat, (real or processed, nutritious or not), you want to make sure that you enjoy them. Don't attempt to eat lackluster foods that you don't enjoy in the name of health. That is not going to serve you and it's not going to be sustainable. Nor is guilting or shaming yourself for eating something that you deem "unhealthy."

Food is life-giving and should be celebrated. Food is our friend, not the enemy. I want you to enjoy eating foods that taste great, make you feel good, and give you energy. Discovering what foods fuel your body is part of your healthy eating journey.

Making delicious, high-quality foods the focal point of your diet, most of the time, is a great practice. These are simply foods that come from the earth or from animals (if you eat them), and not from the factories.

You do not have to become a diehard health nut to eat better or lose weight. But most of us do feel better when we are focusing on real, whole, delicious, high-quality foods. And remember, when you eat better, you feel better.

Feeling good is the name of the game. When we feel better, we make better choices and we take more positive actions with ease. When you find a path that feels good for you, it's going to become much more doable and much more sustainable.

Think about it like this, the more life energy that is in the food you eat, the more life energy you are going to receive from eating that food. This really is the simple basics of eating well. It doesn't have to be more complicated than this. I know our brain wants to make it harder, but gently remind yourself that it can be easier than you may think.

Choose good old-fashioned, real food more often than you don't and if you can cook food at home, even better. Pair that with eating when hungry, stopping when satisfied and being easy with yourself along the journey, and you, my dear friend, have pretty much nailed down the art and science of eating well.

MACRONUTRIENTS

While I am not suggesting you count or manipulate your macronutrients (unless of course you find it helpful), I do think they are worth taking a look at so you can have a basic understanding of how they work.

All of the foods we eat contain nutrients that fall under one of two general categories: micronutrients and macronutrients. Both are essential parts of eating a balanced, nutritious diet.

MICRONUTRIENTS are essentially the vitamins, minerals, and antioxidants found in your food. They are found in real, whole foods and are essential because they protect our bodies from disease, slow the aging process, and they help every system in the body to work properly.

MACRONUTRIENTS are the carbohydrates, proteins and fats found in your food and each plays a different role in the body.

CARBOHYDRATES are the main source of energy for the brain and the body, and offer a variety of vitamins, minerals and antioxidants.

PROTEINS are the building blocks of the body; they support cell tissue growth and repair (muscles, organs, hair, nails), hormone production and increase satiety hormones.

FATS support brain function, hormone protection, increase nutrient absorption and support the immune system.

We happen to live in a world where highly processed, low-quality carbohydrates (think white flour and white sugar) are abundant and seemingly available in excess everywhere you go. This type of carbohydrate makes up most of our modern-day convenience foods as they are the easiest to grab and go.

This is why you hear a lot of people saying that carbohydrates are bad for the body. It's not that carbohydrates are bad for your body (remember, fruits, vegetables, and whole grains are all carbohydrates), it's that the highly processed, highly refined, low-quality carbohydrates that are stripped of all of their nutrients, vitamins, and fiber, when eaten in abundance, are not optimal fuel sources.

These are the types of carbohydrates that cause spikes in insulin, confuse our hormones, and make it hard for us to connect with our natural hunger signals. While they do provide a lot of instant energy for the body, they also provide very little nutritional value, and they tend to leave us feeling unsatisfied and hungry.

Does that mean that you can never eat these types of carbohydrates? Absolutely not (one of my family's favorite meals is my Creamy Butternut Squash Pasta [page 184] made with traditional pasta) but you do want to be aware of how much of them you eat, how often you eat them, and, of course, how they affect your body, hunger and satiety.

The main reason I wanted to address macronutrients is because I often see clients not getting enough quality protein and fat in their diets while having an excess of highly processed, lower-quality carbohydrates.

This combination can make it difficult to feel satisfied and satiated after a meal and often creates strong cravings for sweets while throwing hunger signals out of whack.

A meal that's made up of quality protein, fat, and carbohydrate is going to take longer for your body to break down and assimilate. This type of meal also keeps us feeling fueled and satisfied for longer periods of time which can really help to support health and weight loss goals.

BASIC EATING GUIDELINES

THE **DOS**

COOK OFTEN. The easiest (and tastiest) way to get clean and delicious food into your body is to buy and cook it yourself.

LISTEN TO YOUR BODY. Eat when you are physiologically hungry and stop when you are satiated (so annoying, I know). This can be anywhere between 2 and 6 meals a day depending on what works for you.

FOCUS ON QUALITY. Aim to make the highest quality food choices that are available and affordable.

LOTS OF VEGGIES AND FRUITS. Try to keep things seasonal and local. If you can buy produce from your local farmers market, even better.

SUSTAINABLY SOURCED SEAFOOD. I use the Monterey Seafood Guide to help guide my choices.

LOCAL, ORGANIC AND/OR PASTURED MEAT AND EGGS. Including beef, bison, chicken, lamb, pork, venison, eggs and egg whites.

UNSWEETENED, ORGANIC DAIRY. Milk, yogurt, cottage cheese, and cheese.

100% WHOLE GRAINS. Oatmeal, quinoa, brown rice, sprouted bread, barley, farro, brown rice, lentil and bean-based pastas, wild rice.

HIGH-QUALITY FATS. Avocado oil, extra-virgin olive oil, organic extra virgin coconut oil, ghee, chia, flax and hemp seeds, almonds, walnuts, organic grass-fed butter, all-natural nut and seed butters.

ALL-NATURAL SWEETENERS. Coconut sugar, date sugar, honey, maple syrup, monk fruit, and stevia.

Remember, guidelines like these are tools (not rules) and change takes time—so take baby steps and make them work for you. The name of the game is to eat real, whole, unprocessed foods, as close to their natural state as possible, most of the time.

THE DON'TS

AVOID FRANKENFOODS. Overly-processed, refined foods that are nutritionally void and/or have been created in a laboratory. These foods are always packaged and contain a lot of ingredients.

TRANS FATS AND INDUSTRIAL SEED AND VEGETABLE OILS. Canola oil, corn oil, cottonseed oil, grape seed oil, vegetable oil, safflower oil, sunflower oil, soybean oil, palm oil, and anything hydrogenated or partially hydrogenated.

REFINED GRAINS. White flour and overly-processed breads, cakes, cereals, crackers, cookies, and muffins.

ARTIFICIAL AND REFINED SWEETENERS. Splenda, Sweet 'N Low, Xylitol, high-fructose corn syrup, cane juice and white sugar.

SUGAR-LOADED BEVERAGES. Soda, juices with added sugar, sweet tea, and all energy drinks.

LONG INGREDIENTS LISTS. If buying foods in bags and boxes look for short ingredient lists with words you can recognize and pronounce.

BEING ALL OR NOTHING. Don't tell yourself you'll never eat another donut because it's probably not true. The goal here is progress, not perfection.

DON'T GET FANATIC. Make the best choices you can at any given time and celebrate your wins! Leave all internal criticisms and judgements at the door.

These are examples and not an exhaustive list.

FRIDGE & FREEZER STAPLES

Over the years, I have simplified my eating staples to these lists. Many of my weekly staple ingredients play off of each other to create very simple, nutritious, affordable meals and snacks throughout the week.

When you are building healthier eating habits, letting things be easy is important. When you find something that is easy and enjoyable and that supports your health and weight goals, put it on repeat and keep it as a back-pocket recipe!

FRIDGE STAPLES

- *MY BELOVED CRUDITÉ* Every week, my husband and I chop up a handful of fresh veggies and have them on hand for the week (page 47). Preparing them ahead of time makes all the difference as we find ourselves reaching for them all week long. While we do change things up a bit depending on the seasons and what looks good, our base veggies are chopped broccoli, cauliflower, carrots, celery, fennel, and radishes.

- *DARK LEAFY GREENS.* Sometimes I prepare a big bin of Kale Ribbons (page 48) and other times I buy big bins of pre-washed baby kale or spinach. This changes week to week but we always have prepared greens in the fridge ready to go. I use them in salads, protein shakes, scrambles, and as an easy way to add some vibrant energy to canned soups or frozen pizzas when in a pinch.

- *EGGS AND EGG WHITES.* I usually have two dozen eggs in the fridge ready to roll. One dozen I keep on hand for scrambles, omelets, egg sandwiches and baking. The other I hard boil (page 53) for snack plates and salads. I also buy liquid egg whites to add to my oatmeal (page 64) and for higher protein scrambles.

- *SPROUTED BREAD AND TORTILLAS.* I love good sprouted bread. I prefer them over traditional breads because they are heartier and I find them to be more satisfying. One of my go-to, back-pocket breakfast favorites is toasted bread topped with nut butter and fresh berries or sliced bananas. I also love to make my 2-minute Turkey and Avocado Sandwich (page 138) on raisin bread and often use tortillas for simple quesadillas (page 230) on nights when the kids have different activities.

- *NUT BUTTERS.* We love them all: almond, peanut, cashew—and they are even better when made from scratch (page 44). When buying nut or seed butters, look for all-natural options that list only the nut or seed the butter is made from and possibly some salt. No need for any added sugars or oils!

  We use nut butters in so many ways; they are great with apples and cinnamon, spread on top of a banana, drizzled over oatmeal, mixed into Greek yogurt and added to our favorite smoothies. I also use them as the base for my Gluten-Free Chocolate Chunk Cookies (page 242), so good!

· *PLAIN GREEK YOGURT AND/OR COTTAGE CHEESE.* Both are great sources of protein and I find them really satisfying when I have a sweet tooth because dairy contains natural sugars. I prefer to use 2%, but use whatever you prefer. Mix in some frozen berries, nut or seed butters, or sprinkle on some Stovetop Granola (page 72).

I also love to combine Greek yogurt with Sriracha to use as a dip for quesadillas, tacos and eggs.

· *HUMMUS.* This high-protein, bean-based snack is perfect for dipping your veggies, adding to a sandwich or serving on an after school snack plate with crackers and apples. You can buy so many different flavor varieties at the store or try something new and whip up my Homemade Lentil Hummus (page 89).

· *FRESH BERRIES.* Berries are the one fruit I always keep in the fridge; I find they spoil too quickly when stored on the counter. We enjoy them in oats, mixed in yogurt or cottage cheese, and sprinkled over toast with nut butter. I also love adding them into salads and on snack plates when I want to add extra color and flavor.

· *A VARIETY OF MILK.* We always have some type of milk in the house and usually it's a variety that changes with moods, seasons and what's on sale.

Almond, oat and organic pastured cow's milk are my go-to's. I also keep organic pastured half-and-half on hand for my morning coffee.

· *ROASTED CHICKEN.* Pre-cooked chopped or shredded chicken is a weekly go-to staple. I love to roast my own chicken breasts (page 57) when doing meal prep but if you're in a hurry, a rotisserie chicken can be your best friend. We use this chicken on salads, in sandwiches, to make Chicken Salad (page 124), Quesadillas (page 230), or piled on a snack plate with veggies from our Crudité and dip!

FREEZER STAPLES

· *FROZEN FRUIT.* You will always find frozen berries, mango, pineapples, and bananas in my freezer. We often eat them as a cold and refreshing snack, add them to smoothies and protein shakes, or stir them into Greek yogurt and cottage cheese.

· *FROZEN VEGETABLES.* Picked and frozen in the peak of their season, frozen vegetables are super convenient and budget friendly. Frozen spinach, peas and edamame are some of our favorites. And I always have several bags of cauliflower rice to use in my Overnight Oats (page 66), Baked Buffalo Chicken meatballs (page 224) and Cauliflower Rice Pilaf (page 196).

· *FROZEN RICE.* If brown rice (page 50) or quinoa (page 52) don't make it into my weekly meal prep, I always know that I have backup in the freezer. I love buying frozen brown and jasmine rice to have on hand as an easy and convenient head-start ingredient. You can use them in any recipe that calls for rice, like my Turkey Stuffed Peppers (page 216) or Spinach, Feta, and Brown Rice Pie (page 139). They are also great for creating really quick, last-minute meals—one of my favorites is black beans and rice. Simply heat up some rice from the freezer, mix in a can of low-sodium black beans along with a handful of chopped baby spinach, coconut oil, salt, pepper and garlic powder. Mix that all together and you have a delicious 5-minute meal!

· *ENGLISH MUFFINS.* We keep a variety of sprouted and whole grain English muffins in the freezer at all times. I use them to make my Freezer-Friendly Breakfast Sandwiches (page 82), top them with a little pastured butter or nut butter or spread them with some cream cheese or guacamole and top with a couple of Hard-Boiled Eggs (page 53). And let's not forget about English muffin pizzas. Spread a bit of tomato sauce over a halved English muffin, sprinkle with mozzarella cheese and season with oregano, garlic powder, salt and pepper. Pop in a toaster oven or oven and cook until the cheese has melted and everything is heated through. Serve with some veggies and enjoy!

· *VEGGIE BURGERS.* Frozen veggie burgers are a great option when you have no plans for dinner but still want to make a nutritious choice. Heat one or two up in a pan until warmed and layer on top of an English muffin with avocado and arugula or baby spinach.

· *SOUP OR CHILI.* Cook once, eat twice! Whenever I am making soup or chili I always make extra to keep in the freezer. Perfect for nights when you need something warm, nourishing and already cooked. A great way to save you from ordering takeout.

· *GRAB-N-GO BREAKFAST OPTION.* It's always a good idea to have something on hand for busy mornings. Some of my go-to's include Freezer-Friendly Breakfast Sandwiches (page 82), Cottage Cheese and Blueberry and Oatmeal Pancakes (page 74), and 3-Ingredient Breakfast Cookies (page 70).

· *SWEET TREAT.* I always have one or two of my Clean & Delicious favorites, frozen and on hand for my sweet tooth hits. A few of my go-to favorites include No-Bake Energy Bites (page 236), Chocolate and Avocado Brownies (page 240), Chocolate Chunk Cookies (page 242), and Frozen Banana Snickers Bars (page 244).

· *GRASS-FED AND PASTURED MEAT AND CHICKEN.* I always have ground beef, bison, turkey and chicken breast on hand to pull out for easy meals like my Turkey and Zucchini Skillet (page 222), BBQ Chicken–Stuffed Sweet Potatoes (page 228) and Best Beef Chili (page 178).

· *SEAFOOD.* Frozen salmon and shrimp are always in my freezer. They're both quick cooking and easy to defrost. I am always prepared to make my Crispy Cast-Iron Salmon (page 210) and Garlicky Shrimp with Spinach (page 206) when I have them on hand.

MY GO-TO PANTRY STAPLES

Having a well-stocked kitchen makes eating well so much easier. These are the items I like to have on hand in my pantry to help create simple, clean and delicious meals all week long. Paired with my fridge and freezer staples, I know I can always whip up a simple, healthy meal even when I don't want to try a new recipe.

BEANS AND LEGUMES
Black beans
Cannellini beans
Chickpeas
Kidney beans
Lentils
Pinto beans

CANNED FISH
Sardines
Tuna packed in water
Wild salmon

CANS AND JARS
Diced tomatoes
Pumpkin purée
Chicken, beef and
    veggie Stock
Salsa
Low-sodium soy sauce (or
    coconut aminos)
Full-fat coconut milk

GRAINS AND PASTA
Brown rice
Farro
Oatmeal
Quinoa
Lentil and brown rice pasta

PROTEIN POWDER
Whey protein (vanilla +
    chocolate)*

OILS | FATS | VINEGARS
Extra-virgin olive oil
Avocado oil
Toasted sesame oil
Coconut oil
Ghee
Non-aerosol cooking spray
Apple cider vinegar
Balsamic vinegar
Red wine vinegar

NUTS | NUT BUTTERS | SEEDS
Almonds
Cashews
Macadamia nuts
Walnuts
Pecans
Almond butter
Peanut butter
Cashew butter
Sunflower seed butter
Tahini
Chia seeds
Flax seeds
Pumpkin seeds
Sesame seeds
Sunflower seeds

BAKING ITEMS
Almond flour
Coconut flour
Oat flour
Whole wheat flour
Vanilla
Reduced-sugar chocolate
    chips
Sea salt
Spices
Monk fruit
Stevia
Honey
Maple syrup
Coconut sugar

You can swap in a plant-based protein if you don't eat dairy.

KITCHEN ESSENTIALS

I like to keep things simple in the kitchen; I'm not a fan of unnecessary gadgets and kitchen tools. These are the core kitchen essentials that I use on a weekly and daily basis. Once you have this base set-up, your clean and delicious meals will be a breeze.

CUTTING
Chef's knife
Paring knife
Sharpening steel
Plastic cutting boards
   (for meat and fish)
Wood cutting board
   (for everything else)
Microplane zester
Vegetable peeler
Grater
Spiralizer or Veggetti
   (for making vegetable noodles)

MEASURING
Measuring spoons
Dry measuring cups
Liquid measuring cups

UTENSILS
Rubber spatulas
Wooden spoon
Ladle
Rubber tongs
Whisk
Citrus juicer

POTS AND PANS
12-inch (30.5cm) cast-iron skillet
8-inch (20cm) nonstick skillet
12-inch (30.5cm) nonstick skillet
3–4 quart sauce pan

8-quart stock pot
6-quart Dutch oven
   (for soup and chili)
Steamer basket

BAKING
Rimmed baking sheets
Muffin tin
8-inch (20cm) square baking pan
9-inch (23cm) pie pan
9-inch (23cm) loaf pan
Silicone baking mats
Wire cooling rack

SMALL APPLIANCES
Food processor
High-speed blender
Handheld electric mixer

OTHER
Colander
Fine mesh strainer
Food scale

FINDING YOUR FUEL FOODS

It's important to spend some time noticing what foods fuel your body—I like to call these my fuel foods. Fuel foods are foods that you enjoy, that also nourish, energize, and support your health and weight loss goals. These are the foods that you want to be eating most of the time. And you can only get to know your fuel foods by eating them and noticing how you feel when and after you eat them.

In order for something to be a fuel food for your body, it must meet the following criteria:

- *You must enjoy eating the food.*
- *It must feel good in your body, give you energy and not weigh you down.*
- *It must keep you satiated for at least two hours, and up to five hours.*
- *It must support your health and weight goals.*

Keep in mind that just because someone says a food is healthy does not mean it will feel good in your body, and therefore, it doesn't necessarily mean that it will be a fuel food for you. And on the flip side, just because somebody says a food is unhealthy does not mean that it won't work for you and your body. So be aware of the food rules and the labels that you may have in your head about certain foods and then let your body lead the way.

Plan to keep foods that you love as a part of your long-term strategy. Trying to eliminate all of your favorite foods in an attempt to eat perfectly will always work against you.

Whenever you eat, you want to take notice and check in with yourself.

- *How does your body feel while eating and after eating this specific food?*
- *Do you feel any negative side effects?*
- *Do you have any gas, any bloating? Any digestive upset?*
- *Was the meal satisfying? Is it keeping you satiated for some time after?*
- *Did you enjoy the food?*
- *Would you want to eat this meal again?*

I also want to encourage you to jot down some of the foods that you already know to be fuel foods for your body. Trust what you know to be true for you and for your body. If you have a certain intuition about certain foods or you know that certain foods work for your body, let these foods become your daily staples. This really helps to keep eating easy and enjoyable.

As you identify your fuel foods, jot them down. When you find yourself feeling stuck or confused about what to eat, you can come back to the basics.

2 C & D Basics

Homemade Almond Butter

3 cups raw, unsalted
  almonds

¼ teaspoon sea salt,
  optional

Almond butter is a kitchen staple in our home; we spread it on toast, add it to oatmeal—I even use it as the base for my Chocolate Chunk Cookies (page 242). While I often buy my almond butter pre-made, there's just nothing like making it from scratch—it's healthier, more affordable and superior in flavor to its store-bought counterpart. Plus, it's surprisingly easy to make.

1 Preheat the oven to 350°F (180°C). Place the almonds on a rimmed baking sheet and toast for 10-12 minutes, tossing halfway through, until fragrant.

2 Let the almonds cool for about 10 minutes. You want them to be warm but not fresh-out-of-the-oven hot!

3 Add the warm almonds to your food processor. Blend until creamy, stopping to scrape down the sides as needed. This takes time, so be patient—at first, the almonds will look like almond flour, then they will create a ball in the food processor (take a moment to scrape down the sides and break up the ball), and then finally you will have a rich and creamy almond butter. This can take a solid 15-20 minutes, depending on your food processor or blender.

4 Once the almond butter is smooth and creamy, add in the salt and blend again until well incorporated.

5 Let the almond butter cool to room temperature and then transfer it into a mason jar and seal the lid. Store in your fridge for up to 3 weeks.

**ENJOY YOUR ALMOND
BUTTER IN OR ON THESE
C&D RECIPES:**
Overnight Oats (page 66)
Chia Seed Pudding
  (page 68)
Cottage Cheese, Blueberry
  and Oatmeal Pancakes
  (page 74)
Lentil Hummus (page 89)
Chocolate Chunk Cookies
  (page 242)

**NUTRITION
PER SERVING**
164 calories
164g carbohydrates
6g protein
14g fat
4g fiber

LEVEL UP
Almonds are an energy-dense food that are nutrient-rich and will keep you feeling satiated and satisfied (a little goes a long way!). They are a good source of healthy fats, vitamin E, manganese, magnesium and antioxidants, plus they taste delicious. Be sure to keep them stored in a cool, dry place as the healthy fats in the almond are very delicate.

Add more nutrients and variety to your diet by making a mixed nut butter. Simply sub in raw walnuts, cashews or pecans for some of the almonds and follow the recipe.

Spies Family Weekly Crudité

1 head broccoli, cut into florets

1 head cauliflower, cut into florets

1 bunch carrots, peeled and cut into halves and then thirds

1 bunch celery, trimmed and cut into quarters

2-3 fennel bulbs, trimmed and cut into snack-sized pieces

1-2 bunches radishes, trimmed and halved

Years ago, before we had kids, my husband suggested we cut raw veggies at the beginning of the week to have on hand, since we were both trying to include more vegetables in our diets. He called it our weekly crudité and fast forward to over ten years later we still prepare a big bin (actually two) of washed and prepped veggies every week.

I use these vegetables in so many ways—as a simple snack to serve alongside hummus or white bean dip, chopped into chicken or salmon salad, as the base for soups, tossed into a breakfast scramble, added to a simple salad, and packed into my kids' lunch boxes with some veggie dip.

The veggies listed below have become our weekly staples, but feel free to change it up by choosing some of your favorites. Keep in mind that you can start small. Simply choose 2-3 veggies that you love and slowly build from there.

When you are ready to prep your veggies, turn on some music, grab your favorite knife and get ready to feel great about making your healthy eating intentions a priority!

1 Thoroughly wash all your vegetables before storing.

2 Line a large, airtight container (or two) with a paper towel—this will help to absorb any extra moisture that may develop throughout the week.

3 Layer the prepared veggies in your containers, place another paper towel over the top and pop on the lid. Place in the fridge for up to 7 days.

ENJOY YOUR CRUDITÉ WITH THESE C&D RECIPES:

Lentil Hummus (page 89)

White Bean and Rosemary Dip (page 94)

Collard Greens and Artichoke Dip (page 96)

Rotisserie Chicken Salad (page 124)

Salmon Salad in Butter Lettuce Cups (page 126)

Dairy-Free Broccoli Stem Soup (page 164)

Hearty Minestrone Soup (page 170)

Easy Chicken and Broccoli Quesadillas (page 230)

LEVEL UP ───────────

You will notice that your veggies will lose some moisture throughout the week. If you get to the end of the week and did not finish all your vegetables, or they seem a bit dried out for your liking, no problem! Place them on a rimmed baking sheet, drizzle with avocado oil, season with salt, pepper and garlic powder and roast them in a 425°F (220°C) oven for 20-30 minutes.

Don't toss your broccoli stems! Instead, use them to make my rich and creamy Dairy-Free Broccoli Stem Soup (page 164).

Kale Ribbons

1 large bunch of kale

Simple Kale Ribbon Salad
1 batch kale ribbons,
  see above
1 tablespoon extra-virgin
  olive oil
⅛ th teaspoon sea salt
1 garlic clove, crushed
1 teaspoon fresh
  lemon juice

ENJOY YOUR KALE RIBBONS IN SOME OF THESE C&D RECIPES:
Kale, Quinoa, and Berry Salad (page 114)
Creamy Chicken and Wild Rice Soup (page 174)
Turkey and Butternut Squash Chili (page 176)
Spaghetti Squash with Garlicky Greens (page 188)

LEVEL UP ANY OF THE RECIPES BELOW BY ADDING A HANDFUL OF CHOPPED KALE RIBBONS:
Easy Weeknight Dinner Salad (page 104)
Green Detox Soup (page 162)
Rotisserie Chicken Salad (page 124)
One Pan Creamy Chicken and Artichokes (page 226)
Rainbow Quinoa Salad (page 194)

NUTRITION PER SERVING
87 calories
4g carbohydrates
2g protein
8g fat
3g fiber

You don't have to sit down to a big kale salad to enjoy dark leafy greens throughout the week (although I am sharing one of my favorite simple kale salads here as well!). Simply prepare some kale ribbons when you are doing your meal prep and then work them into your dishes throughout the week. You can add these kale ribbons to soups, salads, frittatas and more!

You can use curly kale or Latino kale (also known as dinosaur kale) to make your ribbons. I recommend trying them both to see if you have a preference.

1 Rinse kale under cold water. Remove stems by holding the bottom of the kale stem in one hand and then use the other hand to pull the leaves up and away. Alternatively, you can fold the kale leaf together and then cut out the stem.

2 Stack 3-4 leaves and roll them into a cigar. Cut the kale into thin ribbons. Repeat until you have worked through all your kale.

3 Place kale ribbons into a salad spinner to remove any excess water. Store kale ribbons in an airtight container lined with a paper towel in your fridge for up to 5 days.

4 Place kale ribbons into a large bowl and drizzle with olive oil. Add salt, garlic and lemon juice.

5 Gently massage all the ingredients into the kale using your hands. If the kale is young and tender, you can simply toss with tongs (no massage required!).

6 Enjoy as-is or add your favorite salad toppings.

LEVEL UP

Save your kale stems! Chop them into little bits and sauté with olive oil, garlic, salt and pepper until tender. They are delicious tossed into scrambled eggs or added to your favorite whole grains.

No time to wash and prepare your kale for the week but you still want to get your dark leafy greens in? No problem! Buy a big bin of pre-washed baby spinach, baby kale or wild arugula and use that as your head start ingredient for the week.

Perfectly Cooked Brown Rice

1 cup brown rice (short, medium or long grain brown rice will work, as long as it's not a quick-cooking variety)

The secret to perfectly cooked brown rice (as in not mushy or undercooked) is to cook it like pasta instead of like rice. Traditionally, rice is cooked with a 2:1 ratio—two parts water to one part rice, but the ratio I encourage you to use is 8:1. Cooking the rice in an abundance of water allows the rice to circulate throughout the pot, thus avoiding a super starchy and/or mushy end result.

1 In a 3- or 4-quart pot, bring 8 cups of water to a boil. Rinse the rice under cold water for one minute, removing any excess starch.

2 Add the rice to the boiling water. Reduce the heat just enough to maintain a steady boil. Boil, uncovered, for 30 minutes.

3 Drain the rice in a fine mesh strainer and then return to the pot. Cover the pot and let the rice rest, off the heat, for 10 minutes. Fluff with a fork and enjoy.

STORAGE Place cooled rice in an airtight container and store in the fridge for up to 5 days.

To freeze your rice, transfer cooled rice into a freezer bag. Use your hands to spread and flatten the rice so it forms and even layer in the bag. Seal shut, squeezing out any excess air. Stack in the freezer for up to 3 months.

How-to reheat frozen rice: Remove rice from the freezer and transfer into a microwave-safe bowl. Cover with a wet paper towel and heat in 1 minute increments until the rice is hot.

ENJOY YOUR BROWN RICE IN OR WITH THESE C&D RECIPES:
Spinach, Feta and Brown Rice Pie (page 139)
Turkey Stuffed Peppers (page 216)
Baked Flounder Parmesan (page 207)
Brown Rice Power Bowls (page 192)

NUTRITION PER SERVING
109 calories
22.9g carbohydrates
2.2g protein
0.8g fat
1.7g fiber

LEVEL UP
The larger the pot, the more evaporation you will have—this is why I like to use a 3- or 4-quart pot. If you are using a larger pot and notice too much evaporation, simply add more water and bring it back up to a boil.

Brown rice is a great head-start ingredient to have on hand for a busy week. You can pair it with any type of protein; think Baked Bone-In Chicken Breasts (page 57), Simply Poached Salmon (page 58), or Crispy Baked Tofu (page 54), and your favorite veggies for a quick and easy meal!

Perfectly Cooked Quinoa

1 cup dry quinoa (any variety)

While usually grouped as a grain, quinoa (pronounced keen-wa) is technically a grain-like seed that is naturally gluten free and rich in protein (1 cup of cooked quinoa has 8 grams of protein)! It's one of the few plant foods that contains all nine essential amino acids and is a great source of nutrients like iron, magnesium, manganese and copper.

Quinoa has a delightful nutty flavor with a light, fluffy texture and it cooks up faster than most grains, making it a great option for busy weekdays. You can find it in a variety of colors, like black, red, white, or a mix of all 3, but each variety cooks up the same way.

If you're trying to find realistic ways to incorporate more nutritious ingredients into your kitchen, quinoa might just be your new best friend. Add this easy, no-fail method to your weekend meal prep to make perfect light, fluffy quinoa every time!

1 Rinse quinoa under cold water before cooking. Keep rinsing until any of the little foamy bubbles that you see are gone and the water is running clear.

2 Combine the quinoa and 2 cups of water in a medium pot. Bring to a boil, cover, reduce the heat, and simmer for 12-15 minutes or until the water has absorbed. When the quinoa is done, it will be translucent and have a little white circle around it (that's the germ).

3 Remove from the heat and let it sit, covered, for 10 more minutes. Fluff with a fork before serving.

ENJOY YOUR QUINOA IN OR WITH THESE C&D RECIPES:
Kale, Quinoa, and Berry Salad (page 114)
The Whole Beet Quinoa Salad (page 116)
Rainbow Quinoa Salad (page 194)
Easy Veggie Fried Quinoa (page 197)

NUTRITION PER SERVING
calories **156**
carbohydrates **27g**
protein **6g**
fat **3g**
fiber **3g**

STORAGE Place the cooled quinoa in an airtight container and store in the fridge for up to five days.

To freeze your quinoa, transfer cooled quinoa into a freezer bag. Use your hands to spread and flatten the quinoa so it forms and an even layer in the bag. Seal shut, squeezing out any excess air. Stack in the freezer for up to 3 months.

How-to reheat frozen quinoa: Remove quinoa from the freezer and transfer into a microwave-safe bowl. Cover with a wet paper towel and heat in 1 minute increments until the quinoa is hot.

LEVEL UP ——————————————————
Simply season your quinoa with salt, pepper, garlic powder and extra virgin olive to create a quick side dish that is packed with flavor. This easy recipe would pair well with buttery Lemon Sole and Spring Vegetables (page x) or One Pan Creamy Chicken and Artichokes (page X).

Easy-To-Peel Hard-Boiled Eggs

12 large eggs

Hard-boiled eggs are one of my favorite ingredients to have on hand for a busy week. They are an easy and delicious way to add extra protein to salads and sandwiches, and can also be enjoyed as is, with a sprinkle of good quality sea salt over the top. There is nothing more satisfying than peeling the shell off your eggs with complete ease, which is exactly what this recipe will teach you how to do.

The secret to easy-to-peel eggs is to shock them in an ice water bath once they are done cooking. It's a fail-proof technique that has never let me down!

1   Lay eggs in a medium-sized pot and add enough water to cover the eggs by about 1 inch (2½ cm). Turn the heat up to high and bring the water to a rolling boil.

2   Shut off the heat, place a lid on the pot and set a timer for 9 minutes.

3   In the meantime, prepare an ice water bath by adding cold water and ice cubes to a large bowl.

4   Drain the eggs and gently place them in the ice water bath where they will rest for 5 minutes.

5   To peel the eggs, tap the egg all around against the countertop to create cracks. Then peel to remove the shell.

ENJOY YOUR EASY-TO-PEEL HARD-BOILED EGGS WITH THESE C&D RECIPES:
Black Bean Breakfast Bowls (page 168, swap out the scrambled eggs)
Easy Avocado, Tomato, and Egg Bowls (page 136)
Simple Romaine Salad with Mint and Dill (page 105, add chopped eggs

NUTRITION PER SERVING
calories **77**
carbohydrates **0.6**g
protein **6.3g**
fat **5.3g**
fiber **0g**

STORAGE   You can store hard-boiled eggs (with the shell on) for up to a week in the fridge. Peeled eggs will last up to 3 days.

LEVEL UP
Look for organic, pastured eggs as an easy way to improve both the quality and flavor of your eggs.

Make an easy breakfast by adding some fresh avocado and sliced hard-boiled eggs over your favorite whole grain toast. Top with everything bagel seasoning for an extra layer of flavor!

Make an egg salad by chopping 4 hard-boiled eggs and combine with 1 tbsp each: finely chopped red onion, finely chopped celery, finely chopped radish. Mix with 1½ tablespoons of mayonnaise or Greek yogurt and season with salt and pepper.

Crispy Baked Tofu Bites

14-ounce (396g) package extra-firm tofu

1 tablespoon low-sodium soy sauce

1 tablespoon avocado oil

¼ teaspoon kosher salt

¼ teaspoon black pepper

½ teaspoon garlic powder

1 tablespoon arrowroot powder

The secret to making tofu so delicious that even your meat-loving friends can't walk away is to make it crispy! A light coating of arrowroot and spices helps to crisp up this recipe while it bakes in the oven. I love using these crispy bites on top of salads and in a quick protein power bowl (page 192) for lunch. It's perfect for meatless Mondays or anytime you want to enjoy a protein-rich, plant-based meal.

1 Preheat the oven to 400°F (200°C) and line a rimmed baking sheet with parchment paper.

2 Drain the tofu and slice into thirds lengthwise so you have 3 even slabs. Lay the slabs on top of each other and slice through them lengthwise to make 3 even columns, then slice across to make 5 even rows.

3 Gently move the tofu to the side and line the cutting board with a lint-free towel or paper towels. Lay the tofu in an even layer on the towel and then top with another towel and some heavy things (I like to stack my cast-iron skillet on top of a baking sheet but anything heavy will do).

4 Let the tofu sit for 15-30 minutes, allowing the liquid to be squeezed out.

5 In a medium bowl combine soy sauce, avocado oil, salt, pepper and garlic powder. Add tofu to the bowl and gently toss until all the tofu is lightly coated with the seasoning.

6 Sprinkle arrowroot powder over the top of seasoned tofu and gently toss together.

ADD CRISPY BAKED TOFU TO THESE C&D RECIPES:
Brown Rice Power Bowls (page 192)
Easy Peanut Soba Noodles (page 190)
Easy Veggie Fried Quinoa (page 197)
Chicken Burrito Bowls (page 132, swap out the chicken)

7 Lay tofu out on your prepared baking sheet and bake for 30 minutes, flipping halfway through.

8 Once your tofu is done it will be crispy and golden brown on the edges. Serve as desired and enjoy.

LEVEL UP ──────────────
Be sure to look for an organic, non-GMO tofu to ensure you are enjoying a high-quality option.

Once the tofu has cooled completely, transfer into an airtight container and store in the fridge for up to 5 days.

Arrowroot powder is a white, powdery starch derived from the arrowroot plant that is naturally gluten free, grain free, vegan, and paleo friendly. If you don't have any on hand, you can sub in cornstarch 1:1.

NUTRITION PER SERVING
195 calories
9g carbohydrates
16g protein
11g fat
0.5 fiber

Baked Bone-In Chicken Breast

4 bone-in split chicken
breasts

1 tablespoon, plus 1
teaspoon avocado oil

2 teaspoons sea salt

1 teaspoon black pepper

1 teaspoon garlic powder

Baking chicken breast with the bone in and skin on ensures that your chicken will be tender and juicy every time. This is a simple but classic technique that I love making when I do my weekend meal prep as it saves time and helps me to prepare easy, healthy meals throughout the week. We use this chicken for soups, salads, sandwiches and snack plates all week long.

Oftentimes, when my kids come home hungry from school, instead of sending them to the snack drawer, I'll serve this chicken right from the fridge with some Lentil Hummus (page 89), sliced cheese, and veggies from our Spies Family Crudité (page 47).

1 Preheat the oven to 350°F (180°C). Place chicken on a rimmed baking sheet and drizzle avocado oil over the top of each breast. Season generously with salt, pepper, and garlic powder both under and over the skin.

2 Bake for 45 minutes, or until the internal temperature reaches 165°F (74°C) and the skin is golden brown. If you cut into the chicken, there should be no pink remaining and the juices should run clear.

3 Cool completely and remove the skin. Chop or shred the chicken breast and store in an airtight container. Chicken will last in the fridge for up to 5 days.

**ENJOY YOUR BAKED
CHICKEN IN OR WITH
THESE C&D RECIPES:**

Rotisserie Chicken Salad
(page 124)

Chicken Tabouli Salad
(page 128)

Easy Peanut Soba Noodles
(page 190)

Brown Rice Power Bowls
(page 192)

Easy Veggie Fried Quinoa
(page 197)

**NUTRITION
PER SERVING**

169 calories

0g carbohydrates

24g protein

7g fat

0 fiber

LEVEL UP

Salt, pepper, and garlic powder will never let you down, but it's also fun to experiment with different flavor profiles!

Mexican Chicken: Rub a mix of 2 teaspoons chili powder, 1 teaspoon smoked paprika, ½ teaspoon ground cumin, ½ teaspoon garlic powder, ½ teaspoon onion powder, ½ teaspoon sea salt, and ¼ teaspoon black pepper over the chicken before baking.

Italian Chicken: Combine 2 tablespoons olive oil, 3 crushed garlic cloves, the zest and juice from 1 lemon, 2 teaspoons dried Italian seasoning, ½ teaspoon sea salt, ¼ teaspoon black pepper. Brush over chicken before baking.

Moroccan Chicken: Rub a mix of 1 teaspoon ground cumin, ½ teaspoon turmeric, ½ teaspoon ground ginger, ½ teaspoon garlic powder and ½ teaspoon ground cinnamon, ½ teaspoon sea salt, ¼ teaspoon black pepper over the chicken before baking.

Simply Poached Salmon

2 cups water

2 tablespoons white
  wine vinegar

1 teaspoon sea salt

¼ cup thinly sliced
  white onion

1 garlic clove, thinly sliced

4 sprigs fresh dill

1 to 1½ lb salmon fillets,
  skin on and pin
  bones removed

1 lemon, ½ sliced into
  rounds and ½ for serving

Black pepper, to taste

Extra-virgin olive oil,
  for serving

This simple and elegant salmon dish is packed with protein and heart-healthy omega-3 fatty acids, while also being quick and easy to make. It's extra moist and tender because it's cooked in liquid with aromatics.

Serve this salmon alongside Popcorn Broccoli (page 144) and Cauliflower Rice Pilaf (page 196) for an easy weeknight meal or add it to your weekend meal prep to help make things easier throughout the week. It can be enjoyed warm, cold, or room temperature—so versatile!

1 Place water, vinegar, salt, onion, garlic, dill, and 2-3 lemons slices in a 10–12-inch (25½–30-cm) sauté pan and bring to a steady simmer over medium heat.

2 Place salmon fillets skin-side down in the pan and cover.

3 Cook 5 to 10 minutes, depending on the thickness of the salmon fillet. The internal temperature of the salmon should be 115°F (46°C).

4 Remove from the pan and season with salt and pepper. Serve with fresh lemon and a drizzle of olive oil over the top.

**ADD SIMPLY POACHED
SALMON TO THESE C&D
RECIPES:**

Salmon Salad in Butter
  Lettuce Cups (page 126)

Brown Rice Power Bowls
  (page 192)

Rainbow Quinoa Salad
  (page 194)

**NUTRITION
PER SERVING**

174 calories

0g carbohydrates

29.3g protein

5.3g fat

0 fiber

LEVEL UP

Look for wild-caught salmon varieties like Sockeye, Coho, King, Pink and Chinook to ensure you are buying the highest quality salmon available.

Use this salmon to create an easy breakfast by layering smashed avocado or cream cheese over your favorite whole grain toast, then top with red onion tomato and salmon.

3 Breakfast

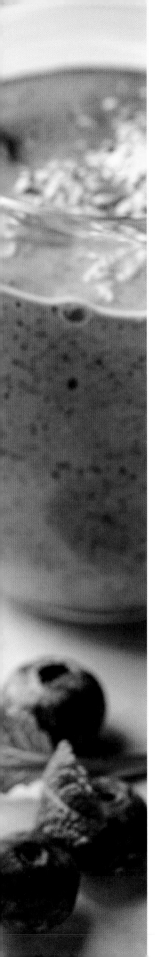

My Go-To Green Smoothie

1 cup baby spinach
½ cup frozen blueberries
¼ cup fresh mint (about 10–15 leaves)
½ avocado
1 Persian cucumber, cut into quarters
1 tablespoon hemp seeds, plus 1 teaspoon, for topping
1 scoop vanilla protein powder
1 cup unsweetened almond milk
4–5 ice cubes

This delicious and refreshing recipe is my go-to when it comes to green smoothies! It's simple to make and packed with protein, greens, healthy fat, and fiber. The fresh mint is a surprising yet delightful addition that gives this smoothie a bright, light, fresh flavor.

1 Combine all ingredients, except the ice cubes, in a blender. Blend until everything is mixed and you have a rich, creamy smoothie.

2 Add the ice and blend again until thick and cold. Pour into your favorite glass and sprinkle with extra hemp seeds.

NUTRITION PER SERVING
337 calories
23g carbohydrates
2g protein
12g fat
11g fiber

LEVEL UP

I love using vanilla whey protein for this smoothie because it adds a rich, creamy texture and ramps up the amount of protein. You can easily swap in a plant-based protein powder if preferred—both are delicious options.

If you don't have protein powder on hand, sub in a few extra tablespoons of hemp seeds instead—they're a great plant-based source of protein and fiber.

Cauliflower Protein Oatmeal

⅓ cup rolled oats

Pinch of sea salt

1 cup frozen cauliflower rice

½ cup egg whites

¼ teaspoon cinnamon

1 scoop protein powder

I've found the secret to making the most delicious, fluffy bowl of oatmeal—and it happens to be loaded with veggies, protein and fiber! It's an unexpected combination of egg whites and cauliflower rice—they add tons of volume and create the best texture as well. I promise, you won't taste either one and you will find yourself satisfied and satiated for hours.

1 Place oats, salt and ¾ cup water in a small pot over low heat and cook for 2 minutes, stirring occasionally.

2 Stir in the cauliflower rice and cook for another 1–2 minutes. You want the oats and cauliflower to warm through, but you don't want them to get too hot. If the oats and cauliflower get too hot, the egg whites will scramble when you add them.

3 Whisk in the egg whites and cook for another 2–3 minutes, continuing to stir periodically. Do this over a low-medium heat so the egg whites temper and become creamy. You'll know the oats are done because they will nearly double in size and will be super fluffy.

4 Transfer to a serving bowl and stir in cinnamon and protein powder. Add your favorite toppings (I love fresh berries and nut butter).

NUTRITION PER SERVING

263 calories

30g carbohydrates

29g protein

3g fat

6g fiber

MAKE AHEAD

You can prep this oatmeal ahead and store it in a sealed container in the refrigerator without the protein powder. Reheat either on the stovetop or in the microwave (for about 2 minutes) with a splash of almond milk or water. Add the protein powder before serving. It will keep in the refrigerator for up to 3 days.

Overnight Oats

½ cup rolled oats

½ cup unsweetened almond milk

¼ cup plain Greek yogurt (or a non-dairy option, if preferred)

1 teaspoon chia seeds

⅛ teaspoon cinnamon

2 teaspoons maple syrup

Fresh berries, fruits, nuts, seeds, nut butter, coconut, cacao nibs, for topping (optional)

Overnight oats are a family favorite in my house! They're one of the easiest, no-cook, make-ahead breakfast options around. I love how versatile they are, and the flavor options are truly endless.

1 Combine all ingredients, except the toppings, in a sealable jar or bowl. Stir until well combined.

2 Cover and transfer to the fridge to soak for a minimum of 2 hours or overnight (for best results, soak for at least 8 hours—this will yield a creamier consistency).

3 When you're ready to serve, top the oats with your favorite toppings and enjoy.

VARIATIONS

Apple Pie and Peanut Butter Stir ⅓ cup diced apple, 1 tablespoon raisins and 2 teaspoons peanut butter into the base recipe before refrigerating.

Tropical Stir ¼ cup diced fresh or frozen mango, ¼ cup fresh or frozen pineapple and 1 tablespoon of unsweetened shredded coconut into the base recipe before refrigerating.

Blueberry and Lemon Stir ⅓ cup mashed blueberries and ½ teaspoon lemon zest into the base recipe before refrigerating.

Peanut Butter and Banana Stir in ½ chopped banana and 1 tablespoon of peanut butter into the base recipe before refrigerating.

Double Chocolate Stir in 1 tablespoon unsweetened cocoa powder and 1 tablespoon mini chocolate chips or cacao nibs into the base recipe before refrigerating.

LEVEL UP

Looking to add more protein to your breakfast routine? Add one scoop of your favorite protein or collagen powder to the base recipe. Easy peasy!

Overnight oats are usually enjoyed cold right from the fridge. If you prefer your oats warm, simply transfer them to a small pot and heat over low for 5 minutes. Alternatively, you could place them in a microwave-safe bowl and cook until warmed through, about 1 minute.

NUTRITION PER SERVING
287 calories
41g carbohydrates
14.8g protein
7.4g fat
5.6g fiber

Chia Seed Pudding

2 tablespoons chia seeds

¼ cup unsweetened almond milk

¼ cup plain Greek yogurt

1 teaspoon maple syrup, honey or sweetener of choice

¼ teaspoon pure vanilla extract

Fresh berries or other fruits, nuts, nut butter, shredded coconut, for topping (optional)

If you've never tried chia seed pudding, now's the time! It's light, creamy, satisfying, and packed with protein, fiber, and healthy fats. It's the perfect healthy breakfast or snack to meal prep, and it's super easy to make.

1 Add all the ingredients to a jar or bowl and stir well to combine.

2 Set the mixture aside for 5 minutes and then give it another stir to break up the clumps of chia seeds. Cover and place in the fridge for at least 2 hours, or overnight.

3 Top with fresh berries or other fruits, nuts, nut butter, or shredded coconut and enjoy. This pudding can be stored in an airtight container in the fridge for up to 5 days.

VARIATIONS

Chocolate Stir 1 tablespoon of unsweetened cocoa powder and 2 teaspoons of cacao nibs or mini chocolate chips into the base recipe before refrigerating.

Matcha & Coconut Stir 1 teaspoon of matcha powder into the base recipe and top with 1 tablespoon of shredded coconut before refrigerating.

Strawberry & Banana Stir ⅓ chopped banana and 3 chopped strawberries into the base recipe before refrigerating.

Peanut Butter & Jelly Stir 1 tablespoon of peanut butter and 1 tablespoon of low-sugar jelly into the base recipe before refrigerating.

Lemon & Raspberry Stir ⅓ cup of fresh raspberries and ½ teaspoon of lemon zest into the base recipe before refrigerating.

LEVEL UP

Milk options: I prefer using almond milk, but whatever milk you have on hand will work. Dairy milk, almond milk, or cashew milk will all make a light, creamy chia pudding. Canned coconut milk will make for a rich and thick pudding.

Yogurt options: 2% Greek yogurt is my go-to, but any Greek yogurt will work.

Low-sugar option: For a low-sugar version, skip the sweetener or use a sugar substitute like monk fruit or stevia.

High-protein option: Protein can help us to feel satiated longer, which is why I often add one scoop (about 2–4 tablespoons) of protein powder to my chia pudding. It also adds another layer of flavor—chocolate and vanilla are my personal favorites!

NUTRITION PER SERVING
206 calories
14g carbohydrates
12.8g protein
11.9g fat
6.2g fiber

3-Ingredient Breakfast Cookies

2 ripe medium–large
bananas

1½ cups quick-cooking
oats

½ cup mini
chocolate chips

These simple little cookies are delightfully delicious and perfect when you need a light and easy breakfast to grab. They're great packed in a lunch box or with a cup of coffee or tea as a snack.

1 Preheat the oven to 350°F (180°C). Line a rimmed baking sheet with parchment paper or a silicone baking mat.

2 Using the back of a fork (or a potato masher), mash the bananas in a bowl until they're broken down. Add in the oats and stir, until a thick cookie batter forms.

3 Mix in the chocolate chips and let the batter sit on the counter for 10 minutes before baking—this allows the oats to soften and makes for more tender cookies.

4 Scoop 1 heaping tablespoon of the batter into your hands and form into a cookie—the cookies will not spread when they bake. Place on the prepared baking sheet and repeat until you have 12 cookies.

5 Bake for 12–15 minutes, or until the cookies are set through and lightly golden brown on top.

STORAGE Keep cookies stored in an airtight container in the refrigerator for up to 5 days.

Cookies can be frozen, fully baked, up to 3 months, then thawed overnight in the refrigerator.

**NUTRITION
PER SERVING**
63 calories
11g carbohydrates
1g protein
2g fat
1g fiber

LEVEL UP

Be sure to use quick-cooking oats in this recipe as they are more finely ground than rolled oats, so they're softer and make for a more tender cookie. In a pinch, you can use old-fashioned rolled oats, which will result in a heartier cookie texture.

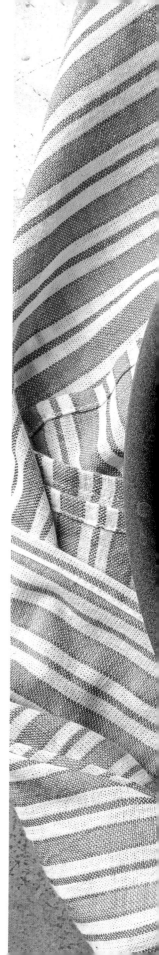

Stovetop Granola

1 tablespoon coconut oil

2 cups rolled oats

⅓ cup chopped walnuts

⅓ cup sliced almonds

½ teaspoon cinnamon

¼ teaspoon sea salt

3 tablespoons
  maple syrup

⅓ cup dried fruit
  (apricots, cherries,
  cranberries, raisins, etc.)

⅓ cup unsweetened
  shredded coconut

This easy granola is sweetened with real maple syrup, naturally gluten free, and perfect for meal prep. While traditional granolas are slow-cooked in the oven, this recipe cooks in just 10 minutes right on your stovetop. I love this granola over a bowl of Greek yogurt with some fresh berries or sprinkled over some apples topped with Homemade Almond Butter (page 44).

1 Heat a large sauté pan over medium heat and melt the coconut oil. Add in oats, walnuts, almonds, cinnamon, salt, and maple syrup. Gently stir until everything is incorporated.

2 Continue cooking for 10–15 minutes, continuously stirring, until oats and nuts are toasty and golden brown. Stir in dried fruit and shredded coconut.

3 Once the oats have cooled, transfer to an airtight container and store in the pantry for up to 3 months.

**NUTRITION
PER SERVING**

171 calories

18g carbohydrates

5g protein

10g fat

3g fiber

LEVEL UP

Once your granola has cooled, stir in a couple tablespoons of hemp seeds for a boost of protein and fiber.

Cottage Cheese, Blueberry, and Oatmeal Pancakes

1 cup rolled oats

2 large eggs or ¾ cup egg whites

1 cup low-fat cottage cheese

1 tablespoon maple syrup

1 teaspoon pure vanilla extract

1 teaspoon cinnamon

Pinch of sea salt

¾ cup blueberries

Unsalted butter, coconut oil, or cooking spray, for cooking

Made with oats and cottage cheese—this is not your typical pancake recipe. Light, delicious, free of all refined flours and sugars and perfect for meal prep. Try doubling the recipe, so you have extra pancakes for busy mornings and make them your own by swapping in your favorite fruit, adding a little lemon zest or mixing in chopped seeds or nuts.

1 Combine all the ingredients, except the blueberries and cooking fat, in a high-speed blender and blend until you have a nice, smooth batter (about 30 seconds).

2 Transfer the mixture into a bowl and gently fold in the blueberries.

3 Heat a large nonstick skillet or griddle over medium-high heat and lightly coat it with butter. Add ¼ cup of the batter to the hot pan and repeat, adding as many pancakes as you can without overcrowding.

4 Cook for 2 minutes, or until the edges start to bubble and the bottoms are golden brown. Flip and cook for another 2 minutes, or until the pancakes are set through and golden brown.

5 Serve with your favorite pancake toppings and enjoy! I like them with a drizzle of nut butter and some extra blueberries.

STORAGE When stored in an airtight container, these pancakes will last in your fridge for up to 5 days and in the freezer for up to 3 months. To reheat, pop them in your toaster oven or microwave until warmed through.

NUTRITION PER SERVING

312 calories

38g carbohydrates

30g protein

4g fat

6g fiber

LEVEL UP

When possible, look for certified organic oats to ensure you are getting the highest quality oatmeal available.

Banana and Oatmeal Pancakes

2 ripe medium-large
  bananas

1 cup egg whites

1 cup gluten-free
  rolled oats

½ teaspoon cinnamon

1 teaspoon baking powder

Pinch of sea salt

¼ cup chopped walnuts

1 tablespoon coconut oil

Banana and oatmeal pancakes are a hearty, healthy, satisfying and family-friendly breakfast. They're also gluten free, sugar free, dairy free and absolutely delicious. If walnuts aren't your favorite, you can swap in other nuts, berries, or chocolate chips

1 Combine the bananas, egg whites, oats, cinnamon, baking powder, and salt in a high-speed blender. and blend until you have a thick batter. Stir in the walnuts or any other add-ins you like.

2 Heat a large nonstick skillet over medium-heat and lightly coat it with coconut oil. Add ¼ cup of the batter and repeat, adding as many pancakes as you can without overcrowding.

3 Cook for 2 minutes or until small bubbles begins to form on the top. Flip and cook for another 2 minutes, until golden brown and set through. Serve with your favorite pancake toppings and enjoy.

**NUTRITION
PER SERVING**

274 calories

30g carbohydrates

13g protein

13g fat

4g fiber

LEVEL UP

This recipe gets all its sweetness from the bananas, so be sure your bananas are super ripe! The riper the bananas, the sweeter they'll be.

If preferred, you can sub in 2 large eggs for the egg whites. Add a small splash of water if the batter seems too thick.

Vegan? Swap in two chia or flax eggs in place of the egg whites. Simply combine 2 tablespoons of ground chia or flax with 6 tablespoons of water and allow to thicken for 5 minutes.

Black Bean Breakfast Bowls

1x 15-ounce (425g) can black beans

½ teaspoon ground cumin

½ teaspoon garlic powder

¼ teaspoon sea salt, plus an extra pinch

1 teaspoon unsalted butter

8 eggs, lightly beaten

¼ teaspoon pepper

1 avocado, pitted and sliced

½ cup Pico de Gallo (page 88) or fresh salsa

Packed with protein and lots of flavor, this black bean breakfast bowl is delicious enough for a weekend brunch and easy enough for a busy weekday morning. It's a super flexible recipe, so make it your own! My son, Jachs, loves his bowl served with cheddar cheese while my daughter, Katie, likes extra Pico de Gallo (page 88).

1 Heat the beans over medium-low heat in a small pot. Season with the cumin, garlic powder, and a pinch of sea salt.

2 Heat the butter in a large, nonstick skillet over medium-low heat. Add eggs, salt, and pepper; cook, stirring occasionally, until eggs are set through.

3 Divide the beans among 4 bowls. Top each with the scrambled eggs, sliced avocado, and Pico de Gallo.

NUTRITION PER SERVING

317 calories

22.5g carbohydrates

21.4g protein

16.2g fat

7.9g fiber

LEVEL UP

Don't have any black beans on hand? No problem! Swap in pinto beans or chickpeas.

Want to add another layer of flavor and nutrient density to this dish? Serve with Perfectly Roasted Sweet Potato Bites (page 156) and top with a dollop of Greek yogurt.

Looking for more green veggies? Scramble your eggs with a handful of chopped baby spinach or Kale Ribbons (page 112).

Asparagus and Goat's Cheese Frittata

1 bunch thin asparagus
  (about 1 lb)
6 whole eggs
4 egg whites (½ cup)
¼ cup 2% milk
½ teaspoon sea salt
¼ teaspoon pepper
1 tablespoon butter
1 small onion,
  finely chopped
3 ounces (85g) goat's
  cheese

This delightful frittata is bursting with fresh flavors from the simple combination of sweet, seasonal asparagus and tangy, creamy goat's cheese. Loaded with protein and veggies, this recipe is ideal as a make-ahead breakfast and works well as a light lunch or dinner. If you have fresh herbs, sprinkle some over the top before serving—fresh dill is my personal favorite.

1 Preheat the oven to 350°F (175°C).

2 Trim asparagus, cut into 1-inch pieces, and steam for 3-4 minutes, or until tender.

3 In a large bowl, whisk the eggs, egg whites, milk, and half of the salt and half of the pepper and set aside.

4 Heat butter in a 12-inch (30.5cm) oven-safe, nonstick or cast-iron skillet. Add the onion and cook for 5 minutes or until fragrant and translucent. Stir in the asparagus and the remaining salt and pepper.

5 Turn off the heat and pour the egg mixture into the pan with the veggies, then top with dollops of goat's cheese. Cook the egg and vegetable mixture in the oven for 18–20 minutes, or until set and lightly brown around the edges.

**NUTRITION
PER SERVING**
240 calories
8.6g carbohydrates
19.4g protein
14.1g fat
1.9g fiber

LEVEL UP

Unlike a quiche, which is baked in a buttery crust, a frittata is crust-less. As a result, it's gluten free, low carb and high protein. A frittata is also much lighter than a quiche without sacrificing any flavor.

If preferred, you can use 8 whole eggs in place of the egg whites.

Freezer-Friendly Breakfast Sandwiches

Cooking spray, butter, or coconut oil

1 teaspoon extra-virgin olive oil

½ onion, chopped

¼ teaspoon sea salt, plus an extra pinch

2 garlic cloves, chopped

2 bell peppers, seeded and chopped

2 cups baby spinach, chopped

⅛ teaspoon pepper

6 eggs

6 whole-grain English muffins (I like using sprouted grain muffins)

6 slices cheddar cheese (or any cheese you prefer)

Making meals ahead of time is often one of the best gifts you can give yourself. This is a recipe you can make over the weekend and keep in the freezer (or fridge) for a delicious and nutritious breakfast when time isn't on your side.

1 Preheat the oven to 350°F (180°C). Spray a 9 x 11-inch (22 x 28cm) casserole dish with cooking spray (or coat with butter or coconut oil).

2 Heat the olive oil in a large nonstick skillet. Add the onion and a pinch of salt. Sauté until the onions are translucent. Add in the garlic and peppers, and cook for another 2 minutes.

3 Add spinach, the pepper, and the remaining salt. Stir and cook until the spinach has wilted. Remove the pan from the heat and allow the veggies to cool to room temperature.

4 In a large bowl, whisk together the eggs and slowly stir in the cooled veggie mixture.

5 Pour the egg and vegetable mixture into the prepared baking dish and bake for 25–30 minutes, or until the center is set and the outer edges are slightly browned. Allow the eggs to cool down and then slice into 6 equal pieces.

6 Separate the tops and bottoms of the English muffins and build your sandwiches by adding one piece of the baked eggs to the bottom of each muffin and topping with one slice of cheddar cheese and the remaining English muffin half.

7 If you're consuming right away, heat the sandwiches at 350°F (180°C) for about 5 minutes or until the cheese melts.

STORAGE To freeze, wrap each sandwich individually in aluminum foil, wax paper, or parchment paper, and place them in a freezer-safe resealable bag. Freeze for up to 1 month.

To reheat, thaw in the fridge overnight for best results. When ready to eat, remove the foil or paper and wrap the sandwich in a damp paper towel. Microwave for 30 seconds, then flip the sandwich and microwave for another 10–30 seconds, or until warmed through. You can also reheat the sandwiches in the oven at 350°F (180°C) for about 10–15 minutes, or in the toaster oven.

NUTRITION PER SERVING
288 calories
31g carbohydrates
14g protein
12g fat
3g fiber

Chicken Apple Sausage Patties

2 tablespoons coconut oil, divided

1 small onion, cut into cubes (about 1 cup)

1 teaspoon sea salt, plus an extra pinch

1 apple, cut into cubes (about 1 cup)

1 lb (454g) dark meat ground chicken

¼ cup chopped parsley

1 teaspoon poultry seasoning

1 teaspoon chopped fennel seeds

½ teaspoon smoked paprika

½ teaspoon pepper

If you enjoy breakfast sausage you're going to love this clean and delicious version. Made with ground chicken, diced onion and apple, this sweet and savory combo creates an addictive flavor profile. I love making them for meal prep, so I can have them for weekday mornings.

1 Heat 1 tablespoon of coconut oil in a large nonstick skillet over medium heat.

2 Add the onion and a pinch of salt. Cook for 2 minutes. Toss in the apple and cook for another 2 minutes or until the apple and onion are tender. Remove from the heat and transfer the mixture to a large glass bowl. Cool at room temperature for 5 minutes.

3 Add the ground chicken, parsley, poultry seasoning, fennel seeds, paprika, pepper, and remaining teaspoon of salt to the bowl. Combine everything together, and use your hands to form 8 equal-sized patties. If the mixture feels sticky, wet your hands while forming the patties.

4 Heat the remaining tablespoon of coconut oil in the pan, and sauté the sausage patties for 4–6 minutes on each side or until cooked through. You'll need to work in batches depending on the size of your pan.

LEVEL UP

If you like sweet sausage, add a couple tablespoons of maple syrup to the mixture. If you like spicy, add 1 tablespoon of diced jalapeños.

Swap the dark meat ground chicken with light meat ground chicken for a leaner sausage patty.

Make these sausage patties ahead of time and store them in an airtight container for up to 5 days in the refrigerator or up to 3 months in the freezer.

Switch up the seasoning by swapping out the parsley with fresh thyme, basil, or rosemary. Better yet, do a combo and make it your own!

NUTRITION PER SERVING

107 calories

6g carbohydrates

11g protein

4g fat

1g fiber

4 Nibbles & Noshes

Mango and Black Bean Salsa

1 cup canned black beans, drained and rinsed

1 large mango, peeled and cut into cubes

½ small red onion, finely chopped

1 garlic clove, crushed

½ jalapeño, seeded and finely chopped

½ red bell pepper, seeded and chopped

2 tablespoons cilantro, chopped

Juice from one lime

¼ teaspoon sea salt

The fresh, vibrant flavors of this mango and black bean salsa are simply addictive! Not only is this a fun and flavorful salsa to serve alongside corn chips, but it's also a great way to add lots of bold flavors to grilled chicken, shrimp, or salmon. If you don't like things with a bit of kick, swap out the jalapeño for green bell pepper.

1 Combine all the ingredients in a medium bowl. Stir well and enjoy immediately or transfer to an airtight container and store in the fridge for up to 3 days.

NUTRITION PER SERVING

51 calories

10.2g carbohydrates

3.1g protein

0.6g fat

2.1g fiber

LEVEL UP

This salsa is super flexible! If you don't have a mango available, use whatever bright, fresh fruit is in season; peaches, plums, papayas, and strawberries would all be delicious.

Make it a meal! Serve this salsa on top of my Easy Chicken and Broccoli Quesadillas (page 230) or make easy tacos by wrapping Simply Poached Salmon (page 58) in corn tortillas and topping with this tasty salsa.

Pico de Gallo

4 Roma tomatoes, deseeded and diced

½ medium white onion, finely chopped

1 jalapeño or serrano pepper, seeded and finely chopped

1 small bunch cilantro, chopped (about ¾ cup)

Juice of 1 lime

½ teaspoon sea salt

Pico de Gallo is a popular Mexican salsa that has a chunky texture and super-fresh flavor. Loaded with fresh tomatoes, onions, jalapeño, cilantro and lime juice, it's an easy and flavorful way to work some extra veggies onto your plate! Be sure to choose beautiful, fresh ingredients for this simple salsa since they truly are the star of the show. I love to serve this salsa alongside some corn chips and it's also delightful spooned over chicken, fish, and eggs.

1   Add all the ingredients into a medium bowl and mix until well combined. Enjoy immediately or cover and refrigerate for up to 3 days.

**NUTRITION
PER SERVING**
51 calories
10.2g carbohydrates
3.1g protein
0.6g fat
2.1g fiber

LEVEL UP
Looking for an easy weeknight dinner? Wrap some shredded Baked Bone-In Chicken Breast (page 57) in a whole grain tortilla and top with shredded cheese and Pico de Gallo.

Lentil Hummus

1 cup brown lentils

¼ cup tahini

¼ cup lemon juice

1 garlic clove

1 tablespoon extra-virgin olive oil, plus extra for drizzling

¼ teaspoon sea salt

¼ teaspoon pepper

2 tablespoons chopped parsley

This protein-packed lentil hummus uses brown lentils in place of chickpeas. Brown lentils are low in fat and extremely dense in nutrients. They are also generally affordable, especially when you buy them in bulk. Because lentils are so small and cook quickly, you do not need to soak them first. Enjoy this hummus with veggies, pita chips, crackers, or as a spread on your favorite sandwich.

1 Inspect the lentils and remove any discolored pieces or small stones. Rinse the lentils under cold water in a fine mesh sieve.

2 Add the lentils and 4 cups of water to a pot. Bring to a boil, reduce heat to a very low simmer, cover the pot with a lid, and cook for 20-30 minutes, or until tender but not mushy. Drain the lentils and leave to cool at room temperature.

3 Place the cooled lentils in a food processor with the tahini, lemon juice, garlic, olive oil, and 1 tablespoon of water and salt. Blend until creamy.

4 Transfer to a serving dish and top with pepper, an extra drizzle of olive oil, and chopped parsley.

LEVEL UP

Lentils are often used in vegan and vegetarian recipes because they are rich in protein (they have 9g per ½ cup), high in fiber, and a great source of quality carbohydrates.

Don't have tahini? No problem, swap in Homemade Almond Butter instead (page 44).

I love having this tasty spread prepared and ready to go for the week. I find myself eating more raw veggies from my Spies Family Crudité (page 46) when I know I have something delicious to dip them in. This hummus will last in an airtight container in the fridge for up to 5 days.

NUTRITION PER SERVING

120 calories

12g carbohydrates

6g protein

6g fat

4g fiber

Guacamole

2 ripe avocados
¼ teaspoon sea salt
1 tablespoon fresh
  lime juice
1 garlic clove, crushed
¼ tablespoon finely
  chopped white onion
¼ cup chopped tomato
¼ cup finely chopped
  jalapeño
2 tablespoons
  chopped cilantro

The secret to making the best guacamole is to keep it simple. Perfectly ripe avocados combined with a handful of fresh chopped veggies, cilantro, lime juice, and sea salt are all you need to make this easy and addictive dip. Serve with corn chips, fresh-cut veggies from your Spies Family Crudité (page 46), or on top of your favorite chili recipe (see pages 176 and 178 for inspiration).

1 Slice the avocados in half, remove the pits and scoop the avocado flesh out of the skin with a spoon. Place in a bowl.

2 Using the back of a fork, mash the avocado against the sides of the bowl until it's rich and creamy. You can make your guacamole as smooth or chunky as you like.

3 Add the remaining ingredients and stir together. Taste and adjust seasoning as desired.

4 Serve with fresh cut veggies and corn chips.

NUTRITION PER SERVING
169 calories
10g carbohydrates
2g protein
0.6g fat
7g fiber

LEVEL UP
When choosing your avocados, check for ripeness by gently pressing the outside of the avocado with your thumb. If there is no give, the avocado is not ripe yet. If there is a little give, the avocado is ripe.

Greek Yogurt Veggie Dip

1 cup plain 2% Greek yogurt

½ tablespoon onion powder

½ teaspoon garlic powder

¼ teaspoon sea salt

⅛ teaspoon pepper

1 teaspoon white wine vinegar

3 tablespoons chopped dill

When I was a kid, there were potato chips and a bowl of ranch dip at all of our family parties and barbecues. So, I decided to level up this classic dip by subbing the sour cream and mayonnaise for thick, creamy Greek yogurt and swapping the store-bought spice packet with my own. This protein-packed dip is perfect served with fresh, crunchy vegetables (pull some out of your Spies Family Crudité, page 46) or alongside your favorite potato chips for a bit of nostalgia.

1   In a medium bowl, stir together all of the ingredients. Serve with your favorite fresh vegetables or baked potato chips.

NUTRITION PER SERVING

48 calories

2.9g carbohydrates

5.9g protein

1.1g fat

0.1g fiber

LEVEL UP ——————————

This recipe works well with nonfat, low-fat, and full-fat Greek yogurt, so choose whichever aligns with your personal and dietary preferences.

Refrigerate leftover veggie dip in an airtight container for up to 5 days.

White Bean and Rosemary Dip

1 large garlic clove

1 teaspoon rosemary, leaves

1x 15-ounce (425g) can cannellini beans, drained

Juice from ½ a lemon

1 tablespoon extra-virgin olive oil, plus extra for drizzling

¼ teaspoon sea salt

⅛ teaspoon pepper

If you like hummus, you'll love this easy dip. Using canned beans keeps prep time quick without sacrificing any flavor. This is the perfect appetizer served alongside fresh veggies (pull out your Spies Family Crudité, page 46) or baked pita chips.

1 Place the garlic and rosemary in a small food processor and pulse, until finely chopped.

2 Add in the beans, lemon juice, olive oil, 1 tablespoon cold water, salt and pepper. Blend until creamy. Add a bit of extra water or olive oil if it's too thick. Adjust seasonings.

3 Transfer the dip to a serving dish and drizzle with olive oil. Serve with pita chips and/or fresh veggies for dipping.

NUTRITION PER SERVING

87 calories

42g carbohydrates

3.2g protein

3.5g fat

5.6g fiber

LEVEL UP

I love the combination of white beans and rosemary, but you can certainly change up the herbs. Parsley, thyme, mint and dill would all be delicious.

This dip will happily last up to 5 days in an airtight container in the refrigerator.

Try adding this dip to your favorite sandwich or on top of a grain-and-veggie bowl. It's an easy way to sneak in some plant-based protein while adding lots of extra flavor.

Collard Greens and Artichoke Dip

1 teaspoon extra-virgin
  olive oil

2 shallots, finely chopped

2 garlic cloves, finely
  chopped

2 bunches collard greens,
  stemmed and
  finely chopped

¾ cup plain nonfat
  Greek yogurt

¼ cup mayonnaise

½ cup grated
  Parmesan cheese

1x 14-ounce (396g) can
  artichoke hearts in
  water, finely chopped

Dash of hot sauce

1 cup part-skim shredded
  mozzarella cheese

Adding collard greens to this creamy and delicious artichoke dip is an easy way to work more dark, leafy greens into your diet. This is a fresher, lighter version of traditional artichoke dip and the perfect make-ahead party snack. I also love to have this on hand as an afternoon snack for when my kids come from school.

1 Preheat the oven to 350°F (180°C).

2 Heat the oil in a large nonstick skillet. Add in the shallots and garlic and cook for 5 minutes, or until fragrant and tender.

3 Add in the collard greens along with a ¼ cup of water. Pop on the lid and simmer until the greens have wilted down. Remove the lid and continue to cook for another 5 minutes, or until all the water has evaporated and your greens are tender. Turn off the heat and cool the greens to room temperature.

4 In a large bowl, combine yogurt, mayonnaise, Parmesan cheese, artichokes, cooled greens, and hot sauce. Mix well.

5 Transfer to an 8x8-inch (20x20cm) oven-safe baking dish. Sprinkle the mozzarella cheese over the top and use a fork to push the cheese into the dip a bit—this will allow the cheese to melt in and on top of the dip.

6 Bake in the oven for 20–25 minutes, or until the cheese has melted and everything is heated through. Serve with tortilla chips and veggies from your Spies Family Crudité (page 46).

**NUTRITION
PER SERVING**
108 calories
4g carbohydrates
8g protein
7g fat
1g fiber

LEVEL UP

While I love using fresh collard greens for this recipe, you can sub in 10 ounces (283g) of frozen greens as well. Just be sure to defrost and drain any excess liquid before stirring the greens into the dip.

This dip can be made up to 1 day in advance and stored in the fridge before baking. Remove the dip from the fridge 30 minutes before you're ready to bake it and allow an extra 10 minutes for it to heat through.

Sweet and Spicy Rosemary Nuts

1 cup raw,
  unsalted cashews

1 cup raw,
  unsalted walnuts

½ cup raw,
  unsalted almonds

½ cup raw,
  unsalted pecans

1 tablespoon
  unsalted butter

2 tablespoon honey

1 tablespoon hot sauce

½ teaspoon sea salt, plus
  extra for finishing

2 tablespoons chopped
  rosemary leaves

Pinch of cayenne
  pepper (optional)

Nuts are an amazing, heart-healthy power snack that can add healthy fat and a bit of protein to your diet. This is a fun recipe to make when entertaining, and it also works well for meal prep. Add these nuts to a cheese board, sprinkle them over your favorite salad, or simply enjoy a handful before heading out for a long walk or hike.

1 Line a half sheet pan with parchment paper and set aside.

2 Toast nuts in a large, nonstick skillet over medium-low heat, tossing occasionally until fragrant and lightly browned. This will take about 5 minutes.

3 Add butter and toss until the nuts are lightly coated. Add in honey, hot sauce, salt and rosemary. Toss again until all the nuts are coated.

4 Transfer the nuts onto the prepared baking sheet, sprinkle with a little extra salt and a light coating of cayenne pepper (if you desire). Cool completely. Store in an airtight container at room temperature for up to 2 weeks.

**NUTRITION
PER SERVING**
199 calories
9g carbohydrates
4.6g protein
17.3g fat
2.1g fiber

LEVEL UP
You can use any combination of nuts that you like, or pick your favorite and just use one variety. Double the recipe if making for a party snack or cut it in half if you're just making them to have on hand for the week.

Roasted Pepper, Goat's Cheese, and Walnut Crostini

1 small sourdough baguette, cut into 10 ½-inch (1cm) slices

2 garlic cloves, 1 whole and 1 finely chopped

1x 12-ounce (340g) jar of roasted red peppers, drained and cut into thin strips

1 teaspoon extra-virgin olive oil

2 teaspoons balsamic vinegar

2 tablespoons chopped parsley

2 tablespoons chopped walnuts

Sea salt and pepper, to taste

4 ounces (113g) goat's cheese

Similar to bruschetta, these simple and flavorful crostini are the perfect bite-sized nosh. I love using store-bought roasted peppers to keep this snack super quick and easy to make.

1 Preheat the oven to 450°F (230°C).

2 Place baguette slices on a rimmed baking sheet and pop in the oven for 5 minutes, or until lightly browned and toasty around the edges.

3 Rub each slice of bread with the whole garlic clove while it's still warm. The garlic will melt into the bread, infusing its flavor and adding moisture to the crostino. Set aside.

4 In a small bowl, combine the minced garlic, sliced peppers, olive oil, balsamic vinegar, parsley, and walnuts. Mix everything together and season with salt and pepper.

5 Spread goat's cheese over the top of each crostino and top with a scoop of the roasted pepper mixture. Repeat until you have worked through all the slices.

NUTRITION PER SERVING
87 calories
9g carbohydrates
4g protein
4.9g fat
.75g fiber

LEVEL UP

Sourdough bread is made via the fermentation of dough, rather than with yeast. Because of this, sourdough has a lower glycemic index than many other breads, making it gentler to digest.

You can prepare the crostini and peppers up to 1 day in advance. Store the crostini in an airtight container and keep in a cool, dry place. Storing the pepper topping in the fridge in an airtight container separarely. Assemble right before serving.

5 Salads

Easy Weeknight Dinner Salad

For the salad

2 romaine hearts, thinly sliced

1 cup thinly sliced red cabbage

1 small or ½ large English cucumber, thinly sliced

1 stalk celery, thinly sliced

1 large or 2 small carrots, peeled and thinly sliced

4-5 radishes, cut into quarters and thinly sliced

½ cup pitted Kalamata olives, sliced in half

¼ cup red onion, quartered and thinly sliced

For the dressing

¼ cup extra-virgin olive oil

¼ cup red wine vinegar

¼ teaspoon Dijon mustard

½ teaspoon dried oregano

¼ teaspoon sea salt

⅛ teaspoon pepper

This is my variation of the salad that was served at the dinner table almost every night of my childhood—it's the one I serve to my family most nights. This is a versatile salad recipe that can easily be adapted to include your favorite salad veggies. I like to serve the dressing on the side, so if we don't finish the salad it will stay crisp and fresh for the following day.

1   In a large bowl combine romaine and red cabbage. Top with cucumbers, celery, carrots, radishes, olives, and red onion.

2   In a small spouted cup or mason jar, combine olive oil, vinegar, mustard, oregano, salt, and pepper. Whisk well to combine.

3   Drizzle the dressing over the salad and gently toss together, or leave it on the side if you think there will be enough for leftovers.

NUTRITION PER SERVING

121 calories

6g carbohydrates

1g protein

11g fat

2g fiber

Simple Romaine Salad with Mint and Dill

For the salad

2 romaine hearts, sliced into thin ribbons

1 cup thinly sliced celery

4 scallions, thinly sliced (½ cup)

¼ cup chopped dill

¼ cup chopped mint

For the dressing

1-2 garlic cloves, crushed

¼ cup lemon juice

¼ cup extra-virgin olive oil

½ teaspoon sea salt

¼ teaspoon pepper

This crunchy, refreshing salad is my take on Maroulosalata, also known as Greek lettuce salad. It's a simple recipe with bright, fresh flavors that is easy enough to make on a Tuesday night, yet delicious enough to serve when entertaining your friends and family. I sometimes swap the celery with fennel and add fresh cucumbers and feta cheese as well. As always, use what you have on hand and make it your own!

1 In a large bowl combine the romaine, celery, scallions, dill, and mint.

2 In a small bowl whisk together garlic, lemon juice, olive oil, salt, and pepper.

3 Drizzle the dressing over the salad and toss until all of the greens have a light coating. Adjust the seasonings and enjoy.

NUTRITION PER SERVING

144 calories

5g carbohydrates

1g protein

14g fat

2g fiber

LEVEL UP

Turn this salad into an easy and elegant dinner by serving it alongside Simply Poached Salmon (page 58) or enjoy it as an easy lunch and top it with a few chopped up Easy-to-Peel Hard-Boiled Eggs (page 53).

Gorgeous Greek Salad

For the salad

2 romaine hearts, sliced in half lengthwise and thinly sliced

1 yellow bell pepper, chopped

¼ cup red onion, cut into quarters and thinly sliced

1 cup cherry tomatoes, sliced in half

1 cup chopped cucumber

1 cup canned chickpeas beans

½ cup pitted Kalamata olives, sliced in half

½ cup crumbled feta cheese

2 fresh peaches or nectarines, cut into bite-sized chunks (optional, but delicious!)

1 avocado, peeled, pitted, and cubed

For the dressing

1 large (or two small) garlic cloves, crushed

1 teaspoon dried oregano

¼ cup lemon juice

¼ cup red wine vinegar

⅓ cup extra-virgin olive oil

½ teaspoon Dijon mustard

¼ teaspoon sea salt

¼ teaspoon pepper

Traditionally a Greek salad is made with chopped vegetables and no lettuce, but I love to use some fresh, crunchy, thinly sliced romaine for the base of this recipe. You will also notice that I suggest the addition of avocado and fresh chopped nectarines (when in season!). While these ingredients are not traditional and completely optional, they really elevate the flavor and texture of this delightful salad.

1 Place romaine in a large bowl or on a large platter. Layer the remaining salad ingredients over the top. I love to do this in a way that displays all the beautiful vegetables.

2 Combine the garlic, oregano, lemon juice and red wine vinegar in a small jar with a lid or a spouted bowl. Add the olive oil and season with salt and pepper. Whisk well or add the lid and give it all a good shake.

3 When ready to eat, drizzle the dressing over the top and enjoy.

NUTRITION PER SERVING

282 calories

17g carbohydrates

6g protein

22g fat

7g fiber

LEVEL UP

You may or may not use all the salad dressing. Any leftover dressing can be stored in an airtight container in the fridge for up to 5 days.

Whenever I work with feta cheese, I look for feta sold in a block form so I can crumble it myself. Feta sold this way does need any stabilizers or anti-caking agents, so the flavor and texture are superior to pre-crumbled feta cheese.

Broccoli Apple Salad

For the salad
6 cups broccoli florets
½ cup shaved carrots
⅓ cup finely chopped
    red onion
1 large apple cored and
    chopped (about 1 cup)
½ cup roasted
    sunflower seeds
⅓ cup chopped
    dried cranberries

For the dressing
¾ cup 2% Greek yogurt
¼ cup mayonnaise
1 tablespoon apple
    cider vinegar
1 tablespoon lemon juice
1 teaspoon honey
½ teaspoon sea salt
¼ teaspoon pepper

This easy-to-make broccoli salad is layered with so many delicious flavors and textures. I've traded out some of the mayonnaise for Greek yogurt, which lightens up the salad a bit while adding a boost of extra protein as well!

1 In a large bowl, combine the broccoli, carrots, red onion, apple, sunflower seeds, and dried cranberries.

2 In a glass spouted cup or mason jar, combine the yogurt, mayonnaise, apple cider vinegar, lemon juice, honey, salt, and pepper. Whisk well.

3 Add the dressing over the salad and mix until everything is well combined and all of the broccoli has a light coating of the dressing. Serve and enjoy.

STORAGE This salad gets even better over time as it marinates in the dressing, which makes it a great option for meal prep. You can make it up to 8 hours before you plan to serve it or store the salad in an airtight container for up to 4 days.

NUTRITION PER SERVING
228 calories
23g carbohydrates
8g protein
13g fat
5g fiber

LEVEL UP ─────────────────────────────

If you're sensitive to raw vegetables, lightly steam or blanch the broccoli before assembling the salad.

You can use any variety of apple or this easy salad, but my personal favorite is Honey Crisp. They are the perfect combination of sweet and tart with a super-crunchy texture that pairs really well with this salad.

Harvest Salad

For the sweet potatoes
1 sweet potato,
  peeled and cut into
  ½-inch cubes
1 tablespoon avocado oil
½ teaspoon curry powder
½ teaspoon garlic powder
½ teaspoon sea salt
½ teaspoon pepper

For the dressing
¼ cup tahini
1 tablespoon maple syrup
1 garlic clove, crushed
1 tablespoon apple
  cider vinegar
1½ tablespoons
  lemon juice
¼ teaspoon sea salt
  and pepper

For the salad
8 ounces (226g) mixed
  salad greens
2 rainbow carrots, tops
  removed and sliced
  into rounds
5-6 radishes, tops
  removed and sliced
  into rounds
1 small green apple, sliced
⅓ cup Sweet and Spicy
  Rosemary Nuts
  (page 98)
¼ cup pumpkin seeds
1 avocado, peeled, pitted,
  and finely chopped
⅓ cup pomegranate arils

Loaded with gorgeous autumn fruits and vegetables and drizzled with a tahini and maple dressing that you may be tempted to eat with a spoon, this combination of flavors and textures will have your non-salad-loving friends asking for the recipe.

1 Preheat your oven to 425°F (220°C). Toss the sweet potato with the avocado oil, curry powder, garlic powder, salt, and pepper.

2 Arrange the sweet potatoes in a single layer on a rimmed baking sheet and roast for 30 minutes, flipping halfway through. Remove from the oven and cool to room temperature.

3 In the meantime, combine the tahini, maple syrup, crushed garlic, apple cider vinegar, lemon juice, salt, pepper, and ¼ cup of water in a small bowl or spouted cup. Whisk until loose, creamy, and well combined.

4 Spread the mixed greens out on a large serving plate. Layer the carrots, radishes, apple, sweet potato, nuts, pumpkin seeds, avocado, and pomegranate arils.

5 Drizzle with tahini and maple dressing and enjoy.

*If you don't have any Sweet and Spicy Rosemary Nuts made, you can swap in walnuts, pecans, almonds, or cashews.

NUTRITION PER SERVING
409 calories
38g carbohydrates
9g protein
28g fat
9g fiber

LEVEL UP
This is a super flexible salad that can easily work with a variety of fruits and vegetables. No pomegranate? Swap in dried cranberries or goji berries. No apple? Swap in pear. No mixed greens? Swap in kale. No sweet potatoes? Try butternut squash. You get the idea... Make this salad work for you and whatever fruits and veggies you have on hand.

Shredded Kale and Brussels Salad with Green Olives and Parmesan

For the salad

4 cups Kale Ribbons (page 47)

2 cups thinly sliced Brussels sprouts

⅓ cup thinly sliced celery

⅓ cup thinly sliced scallions

½ cup toasted pecans

1 cup large pitted green olives, thinly sliced

½ cup shaved Parmesan cheese

Cracked pepper, to taste

For the dressing

1 garlic clove, crushed

¼ cup lemon juice

¼ cup extra-virgin olive oil

1 tablespoon tahini

1 teaspoon honey

¼ teaspoon sea salt

If my husband could eat one salad for the rest of his life, this would be the one (and I totally understand why). This is a hearty salad that could easily take the place of any side dish on a holiday table, but is simple enough for a busy weeknight. If you are trying to get more dark leafy greens into your diet, this gorgeous salad is a very delicious way to do just that.

1 In a large shallow bowl, combine the kale and Brussels sprouts. Layer the celery, scallions, pecans, and olives.

2 In a small jar or spouted glass cup, combine the garlic, lemon juice, olive oil, tahini, honey, and salt. Whisk well.*

3 Drizzle the dressing over the top and gently toss everything together, coating all of the ingredients with a light layer of dressing (I find it easiest to do this with my hands). Top with shaved Parmesan cheese and black pepper.

*You will notice that this salad is very lightly dressed, which I do intentionally to help balance the richness of the olives, pecans, and cheese. However, if you would like a bit of extra dressing, simply increase the lemon juice and olive oil to ⅓ cup each.

NUTRITION PER SERVING

380 calories

14g carbohydrates

10g protein

34g fat

7g fiber

LEVEL UP

You can easily turn this salad into a main meal by topping it with shredded Baked Bone-in Chicken Breast (page 57) or Simply Poached Salmon (page 58). If you want to keep the meal 100% plant-based, top it with a scoop of Perfectly Cooked Quinoa (page 52) or Crispy Baked Tofu (page 54).

Kale, Quinoa, and Berry Salad

For the dressing

¼ cup extra-virgin olive oil

¼ cup lemon juice

1 teaspoon honey

1 small garlic
clove, crushed

¼ teaspoon sea salt

⅛ teaspoon pepper

For the salad

1 batch Kale Ribbons
(about 6 cups) (page 47)

1 cup Perfectly Cooked
Quinoa (page 52),
cooled

1x 15-ounce (425g) can
chickpeas, drained
and rinsed

1 cup blueberries

3 ounces (85g) feta
cheese, crumbled

¼ cup chopped unsalted
roasted almonds

1 avocado, peeled, pitted
and chopped

This kale and quinoa salad is a nutritional powerhouse that also happens to have a delightful balance of flavors and textures. The tangy feta paired with the savory almonds and sweet, tart berries creates a little party in your mouth. I love watching both of my kids pile this salad onto their plates.

1 Whisk together the olive oil, lemon juice, honey, garlic, salt, and pepper.

2 Place kale in a large bowl and gently toss with the dressing. Top with cooked quinoa, chickpeas, blueberries, feta, almonds, and avocado. Gently combine and enjoy!

**NUTRITION
PER SERVING**

471 calories

40.8g carbohydrates

15.2g protein

30.2g fat

11.8g fiber

LEVEL UP ———————

If you plan to make this salad ahead of time, don't add the avocado until you are ready to serve, as it will brown.

Any type of berry would be delicious in this salad.

Add a boost of lean protein to this meal by topping this salad with shredded Baked Bone-in Chicken Breast (page 57).

The Whole Beet Quinoa Salad

4 medium beets, with the greens attached

2 teaspoons extra-virgin olive oil

3 garlic cloves, finely chopped

Salt and pepper, to taste

½ red onion, finely chopped

1 teaspoon apple cider vinegar

2 tablespoons chopped dill

1 cup Perfectly Cooked Quinoa (page 52), cooled

2 ounces (56g) feta cheese, crumbled

This bright, beautiful dish uses both the root and the leaves of the beet to create an earthy, flavorful quinoa salad that is nutritious and delicious. If you've ever worked with red beets before, you know very well that unless you are wearing gloves, your hands will turn the same brilliant red color that penetrates the beet, so keep that in mind when you choose your cutting board (and your t-shirt).

1 Preheat the oven to 375°F (190°C).

2 Separate the stems from the beet greens. Finely chop the stems and coarsely chop the leaves. Set aside.

3 Trim and peel the beet roots and then cut them into small bite-sized pieces (wear gloves if you want). Toss with one teaspoon of olive oil, plus the garlic, salt, and pepper.

4 Place the beets roots on a rimmed baking sheet and roast for 30 minutes, or until they are fork-tender.

5 While the beet roots are cooking, heat the remaining oil in a large skillet over medium heat. Reserve 2 tablespoons of onion and add the remainder along with the beet stems to the pan. Cook, stirring, for 4-5 minutes or until tender.

6 Add the beet greens, apple cider vinegar, a few pinches of salt and pepper, and sauté, tossing, until just wilted. Allow everything to cool a bit.

7 In a large bowl, combine the reserved onions, dill, beet greens, roasted beets, and quinoa. Season with salt and pepper. Gently toss everything together, top with crumbled feta cheese, adjust seasonings and serve.

NUTRITION PER SERVING
10 calories
14g carbohydrates
4g protein
4g fat
3g fiber

LEVEL UP

Beets are loaded with amazing nutrients, they're rich in potassium, manganese and folate as well as vitamins A, B6, C, and K. They are low calorie and said to be good for the heart and have anti-inflammatory properties. Beets are also high in fiber, which can help with digestion.

Mediterranean Chickpea Salad

For the salad

2x 15-ounce (425g) cans chickpeas, drained and rinsed

1 English cucumber, chopped

½ cup finely chopped red onion

2 bell peppers, (1 yellow plus 1 orange, ideally), chopped

½ cup pitted Kalamata olives, sliced in half

4 ounces (113g) feta cheese, crumbled

1 avocado, peeled, pitted and, chopped

2 tablespoons chopped mint

2 tablespoons chopped basil

For the dressing

¼ cup extra-virgin olive oil

¼ cup fresh lemon juice

½ teaspoon Dijon mustard

1 large garlic clove, crushed

½ teaspoon sea salt

¼ teaspoon pepper

This is a light, bright, budget-friendly salad that is easy to make. Chickpeas are combined with cucumbers, bell pepper, red onion, olives, avocado, feta, and fresh herbs for a salad that is hearty enough for a lovely lunch and equally perfect for dinner or a cookout.

1 Add all of the salad ingredients to a large bowl and set aside.

2 Add all of the dressing ingredients to a small spouted cup or jar and whisk until well combined, or add the lid to the jar and give it a good shake.

3 Drizzle the dressing over the salad and gently toss until all the beans and veggies are coated. Adjust seasonings and enjoy.

LEVEL UP

Choose an avocado that is just ripe and not too soft. If you're not eating this salad right away, leave the avocado out and add it in right before serving.

Store this salad in an airtight container and keep it in the fridge for up to 5 days.

If you don't want to be bothered with chopping fresh herbs, sub in one tablespoon of dried herbs (oregano, basil, and mint would all work well).

Turn this salad into a protein-packed lunch by adding in a couple of Easy-to-Peel Hard-Boiled Eggs (page 53).

NUTRITION PER SERVING
169 calories
10g carbohydrates
3g protein
1g fat
4g fiber

Deconstructed Pesto Potato Salad

1 lb small, thin-skinned yellow potatoes, rinsed and quartered

1 lb green beans, trimmed and cut into 1-inch pieces

4–6 garlic cloves, crushed

½ cup finely chopped basil

¼ cup toasted pine nuts

¼ cup extra-virgin olive oil

Salt and pepper, to taste

This beautiful potato salad captures all the bright, vibrant flavors of pesto without you having to make pesto. Simply chop up the classic pesto ingredients: basil, garlic, and pine nuts and toss with baby potatoes and green beans. Finish with the best extra-virgin olive oil you have on hand and a hearty pinch of sea salt and enjoy. This salad makes a great side dish and is equally tasty served for breakfast with an over-easy egg on top.

1 Bring the potatoes to a boil in a large pot of salted water. Once the water is boiling, allow the potatoes to cook for another 5 minutes or so, until almost tender. Right before the potatoes are ready, toss in the green beans and cook for 2 more minutes, or until the beans are nice and bright and and a knife will easily pierce through the potatoes.

2 Drain the potatoes and beans in a colander. Place everything back into the warm pot.

3 Stir in the garlic, basil, pine nuts, olive oil, salt, and pepper and mix together thoroughly. Taste for seasoning (this salad tends to beg for a couple extra pinches of salt).

NUTRITION PER SERVING
196 calories
19g carbohydrates
4g protein
13g fat
4g fiber

LEVEL UP ────────────────
If you can't find toasted pine nuts, you can easily toast them yourself. Heat a small nonstick pan over low heat and add the pine nuts to the dry pan. Toast for 3–5 minutes, stirring along the way, until lightly golden and fragrant.

Lightly toasted walnuts or almonds are a great substitute for the pine nuts in this salad.

6 Easy Lunches

Rotisserie Chicken Salad

2 cups chopped rotisserie chicken or Baked Bone-In Chicken Breast (page 54), cooled

⅓ cup finely chopped celery

⅓ cup finely chopped radish

⅓ cup finely chopped red onion

1 cup chopped baby spinach

⅓ cup 2% Greek yogurt

⅓ cup mayonnaise

½ teaspoon sea salt

¼ teaspoon pepper

I love a good shortcut and this dish is just that! Combine store-bought or meal-prepped chicken (page 54) with your favorite veggies and mix with mayonnaise and Greek yogurt to create a bright, fresh, creamy chicken salad in just minutes. This is a quick and easy lunch idea that's delicious served in a sandwich, with a side of crackers or in crisp lettuce cups.

1 Combine all of the ingredients in a large bowl and mix until everything is combined.

2 Serve with crackers, on top of whole-grain bread, wrapped in lettuce cups, or over your favorite salad.

LEVEL UP

When you do your grocery shopping, pick up a rotisserie chicken and shred it while it's still warm (this makes it super easy to do!). Store the prepared chicken in an airtight container in your refrigerator to have on hand for the week. You can use it to top salads, stuff into tacos, make quesadillas, or to make this salad.

Make this chicken salad dairy-free by using mayonnaise in place of the yogurt.

LEVEL UP

Look for a high-quality mayonnaise that uses avocado oil or olive oil as the base.

To create a higher protein, lower fat chicken salad, use all Greek yogurt in place of the mayo.

Think outside the box! Go beyond onions and celery by adding your favorite fresh crunchy veggies to this chicken salad. Chop up extra veggies from your Spies Family Crudité (page 47).

NUTRITION PER SERVING
165 calories
2g carbohydrates
15g protein
11g fat
1g fiber

Salmon Salad in Butter Lettuce Cups

2x 6-ounce (170g) cans
  wild salmon, drained

1 celery stalk,
  finely chopped

¼ red onion,
  finely chopped

1 Persian cucumber,
  finely chopped

2 tablespoons
  chopped capers

2 tablespoons mayonnaise

2 tablespoons plain
  nonfat Greek yogurt

¼ teaspoon sea salt, plus
  more to taste

⅛ teaspoon pepper, plus
  more to taste

2 tablespoons chopped
  herbs (I like dill and
  parsley) (optional)

8 butter lettuce
  leaves, washed

Canned salmon makes a great pantry staple; it's an easy way to keep a high-quality protein source on hand. While we love this salmon salad wrapped in tender butter lettuce cups, it's also delicious served over a green salad, alongside some crackers, or loaded onto your favorite whole-grain bread.

1 In a large bowl, combine the salmon, celery, red onion, cucumbers, capers, mayonnaise, Greek yogurt, salt, pepper, and fresh herbs (if using). Stir to combine.

2 Place a scoop of salmon salad into each butter lettuce cup. Sprinkle the cups with extra herbs and black pepper.

STORAGE This salmon salad will last up to 3 days in your fridge when stored in an airtight container.

**NUTRITION
PER SERVING**
517 calories
57g carbohydrates
42g protein
17g fat
15g fiber

LEVEL UP
If you have time to plan ahead, make this recipe with homemade Simply Poached Salmon (page 58). It only takes 15 minutes to make and is a great ingredient to add to your weekend meal prep.

If you want to keep this recipe dairy free, use all mayonnaise and skip the yogurt.

If you want to lighten things up and add a bit more protein, skip the mayo and use all Greek yogurt.

Chicken Tabouli Salad

½ cup bulgur wheat

2 garlic cloves, minced

½ cup chopped flat
  leaf parsley

¼ cup chopped mint

½ cup sliced scallions

1 tomato, diced

2 tablespoons fresh
  lemon juice

2 tablespoons extra-virgin
  olive oil

Sea salt and pepper,
  to taste

1 cup shredded Baked
  Bone-in Chicken Breast
  (page 54), or rotisserie
  chicken

1x 15-ounce (456g) can
  chickpeas drained
  and rinsed

Tabouli (or tabbouleh), is a popular Middle Eastern salad made up of bulgur wheat, finely chopped vegetables, and fresh herbs, all tossed with extra-virgin olive oil and lemon juice. While I use this base as my inspiration, I love to bump up the protein by adding baked chicken and chickpeas, amplifying this beautiful side salad to a healthy main dish that works perfectly as a make-ahead lunch.

I usually make this with my Baked Bone-in Chicken Breasts (page 54) but when in a pinch, store-bought rotisserie chicken works really well.

1 Bring 1 cup of water to a boil in a medium saucepan and stir in the bulgur wheat. Bring back to a boil, reduce the heat, cover and simmer for about 10–15 minutes, or until all the water has been absorbed.

2 In a large bowl, combine the garlic, parsley, mint, scallions, and tomato. Stir in the cooled bulgur, lemon juice and olive oil. Season with salt and pepper.

3 Gently toss in the chicken and the chickpeas, adjust your seasonings and enjoy.

**NUTRITION
PER SERVING**

305 calories

45g carbohydrates

22g protein

5g fat

12g fiber

LEVEL UP ─────────────
Bulgur is made from whole wheat berries that have been steamed, cooked, dried, and cracked. They come in fine, medium and coarse grain. You want to use fine grain whenever making tabouli salad. Bulgur is said to support digestive health while helping to balance blood sugar.

Tuna Pasta Salad

12 ounces elbow pasta

1 cup finely chopped
   red onion

1 cup finely
   chopped celery

2x 5-ounce (141g) cans
   tuna packed in
   water, drained

1 cup frozen
   peas, defrosted

2 tablespoons mayonnaise

½ cup plain nonfat
   Greek yogurt

1 tablespoon red
   wine vinegar

Sea salt and pepper,
   to taste

When I was growing up, my older sister, Kristi, would make her version of this tuna pasta salad on a weekly basis. It was always one of my favorites, so I wanted to find a way to level-up some of the ingredients. I've cut back on the mayo by adding in Greek yogurt and added an extra pop of color and texture with the peas. While I don't make a lot of recipes that use refined flour, this is a dish that my family and I prefer using traditional white pasta in. I find it much easier to stick to a healthy lifestyle when I am not restricting or completely eliminating food groups from my diet and this recipe is a perfect example of that. If, however, you are gluten-free, brown rice elbows are a great option.

1 Cook pasta according to package directions. Drain and rinse under cold water to stop the noodles from cooking further.

2 In a large bowl, combine cooked pasta, onion, celery, tuna, peas, mayonnaise, Greek yogurt, vinegar, salt, and pepper. Stir well and enjoy.

**NUTRITION
PER SERVING**

355 calories

59g carbohydrates

17g protein

5g fat

4g fiber

LEVEL UP

When stored in an airtight container, this pasta salad will last up to 5 days in the fridge.

To keep this recipe dairy free, skip the yogurt and use all mayo.

To lower the fat and increase the protein, skip the mayo and use all yogurt.

Look for skipjack tuna as it has the lowest levels of mercury when compared to other canned tuna options.

Chicken Burrito Bowls

1 tablespoon extra-virgin olive oil

1 garlic clove, chopped

4 cups cauliflower rice (no need to defrost)

Salt and pepper, to taste

¼ cup low-sodium chicken broth

¼ cup chopped scallions

¼ cup chopped cilantro

1 tablespoon fresh lime juice

1¼ lbs ground chicken

2 tablespoons taco seasoning

1x 15-ounce (425g) can black beans, drained and rinsed

2 cups frozen corn, defrosted

1 pint cherry tomatoes, quartered

Optional sauce

½ cup plain nonfat Greek yogurt

1 tablespoon chipotle sauce (reserved from 1 can chipotles in adobo)

1 teaspoon fresh lime juice

NUTRITION PER SERVING
517 calories
57g carbohydrates
42g protein
17g fat
15g fiber

These chicken burrito bowls taste way better than anything you can buy pre-made They're also more nutritious and so easy to make. I like to prepare them on the weekend when I am doing my meal prep, so I have them ready to go for lunch during the week.

1 Heat 1 teaspoon of the oil in a large nonstick skillet, toss in the garlic with a pinch of salt and sauté until fragrant.

2 Add the cauliflower rice to the pan along with salt, pepper and chicken broth. Pop on the lid and cook for 4–5 minutes, or until the cauliflower rice is tender.

3 Transfer the cauliflower rice to a bowl and allow to cool before stirring in the scallions, cilantro, and lime juice. Set aside.

4 Heat a large nonstick skillet over medium heat, and add in the remaining oil and ground chicken. Season with salt and pepper and break into crumbles with a rubber or wooden spatula.

5 Once the chicken has turned from translucent to opaque, add in the taco seasoning and stir to coat the chicken with the spices. Cook for a couple more minutes or until chicken is cooked through. Shut off the heat and let it cool.

6 Starting on one side of your meal prep container, layer the cauliflower rice, corn, black beans, chicken and tomatoes. Repeat until you make 4 burrito bowls.

SAUCE —————————————————

Combine the Greek yogurt, chipotle sauce, and lime juice. Mix well and when ready to eat, top each bowl with a drizzle of this cool and creamy sauce.

LEVEL UP —————————————————

You can eat these burrito bowls at any temperature. I often eat them straight from the fridge.

Got leftover chipotles in adobo sauce? Place the remaining contents in a food processor and purée until it looks like a paste. Add a spoonful to each section of an ice cube tray and freeze until solid. Transfer the cubes into a freezer-friendly bag and return them to the freezer. Add to your favorite soups, stews, and chilis to create a warm, smoky flavor.

Bison Taco Salad Bowls

1 lb ground bison

1 teaspoon extra-virgin olive oil

2 medium bell peppers (1 red and 1 green), seeded and chopped

½ medium onion, chopped

3 garlic cloves, finely chopped

3 tablespoons taco seasoning

½ cup low-sodium beef broth

1x 15-ounce (425g) can kidney beans, drained and rinsed

Sea salt and pepper, to taste

3 cups Perfectly Cooked Brown Rice (page 51)

½ cup part-skim shredded cheddar cheese

1 large romaine heart, thinly sliced

½ medium tomato, finely chopped

Ground bison is a lean source of high-quality protein that is rich in vitamin B12, zinc, selenium and iron. Bison is also lower in fat and cholesterol than ground beef. It has a flavor that is similar to beef, but milder and sweeter. This is the perfect lunch to meal prep for a busy week as it's delicious, nutritious and full of flavor, plus it will last in the fridge for up to 5 days.

1   Heat a large nonstick skillet pan over medium-high heat. Add the bison to the dry pan, then using a wooden or rubber spatula, break the meat apart. Cook until the meat is no longer pink.

2   Push the meat to one side of the pan. Add the olive oil to the empty half of the pan, then add in the peppers, onion, garlic, and a pinch of salt. Allow the veggies to cook until they are tender, about 5 minutes.

3   Combine the meat and the veggies. Stir in the taco seasoning to evenly coat the mixture. Stir in the broth and beans and allow to cook until the broth has evaporated and the beans are heated through, another 5 minutes or so.

4   Put a ½ cup of brown rice in the bottom of each serving bowl. Top with a small handful of romaine, a heaping tablespoon of cheese, and one cup of the bison-veggie mixture. Sprinkle with chopped tomatoes and enjoy.

STORAGE Taco bowls will last up to 5 days in the refrigerator. The cooked ingredients can be stored together (bison and rice). This will allow you to conveniently reheat them in the microwave. I suggest storing the chilled components in separate containers (lettuce, cheese and tomatoes), so they will stay as fresh as possible.

NUTRITION PER SERVING
325 calories
29g carbohydrates
20g protein
14g fat
4g fiber

LEVEL UP

You can use any type of ground meat that you enjoy for this recipe. Ground beef, turkey, and/or chicken would all be great options. If you want a plant-based bison bowl, swap the meat for Crispy Baked Tofu (page 57).

Add another layer of flavor to your taco bowl by topping them with Pico de Gallo (page 88) or Guacamole (page 90).

Easy Tomato and Avocado Egg Bowls

2 ripe tomatoes, cut into chunks

1 avocado, peeled, pitted and cut into chunks

2 Persian cucumbers, quartered and sliced

4 Easy-to-Peel Hard-Boiled Eggs (page 53), peeled and cut into bite-sized chunks

4 teaspoons extra-virgin olive oil

½ teaspoon sea salt

¼ teaspoon pepper

1 teaspoon chopped herbs, like mint, basil or cilantro (optional)

I first enjoyed this easy lunch bowl when my friend Julie made it for me after a yoga class, and I was delighted at how insanely delicious such a simple meal could be. It's packed with protein, fiber, and healthy fats, which help to keep you feeling satiated and satisfied for hours. If you meal prep your eggs (which I always do) this nutritious lunch comes together in just minutes!

1 Divide the tomatoes, avocado, cucumber, and eggs among 2 bowls. Drizzle the olive oil over the top and season with salt and pepper. Finish with fresh herbs, if using, and enjoy.

NUTRITION PER SERVING

417 calories
17g carbohydrates
16g protein
7g fat
8g fiber

LEVEL UP ——————————————

Lighten this recipe up a bit by subbing out 1 hard-boiled egg with 2 hard-boiled egg whites. This cuts back on the fat while adding an extra boost of protein.

I also love this recipe with canned tuna in olive oil. Simply swap out the eggs with the tuna—no need to add extra oil.

Turkey and Avocado Super Sandwich

4 slices sprouted
  raisin bread
1 garlic clove
6 slices organic
  turkey breast
1 avocado, peeled
  and pitted
¼ teaspoon sea salt

This sandwich is proof that enjoying a healthy lunch can be quick, easy and insanely delicious! While this sandwich may not seem like much, the sweet-and-salty combination of the raisin bread, turkey, and avocado creates a flavor explosion that tastes like a party in your mouth.

1 Lightly toast the bread until golden brown. Rub each slice of toast with the garlic clove allowing the garlic to melt into the bread.

2 Mash the avocado in a small bowl with the back of a fork and season with salt.

3 Divide the avocado over the top of 2 pieces of the toast. Layer 3 slices of turkey on each avocado toast and then top with the remaining toasted bread. Slice in half and enjoy!

**NUTRITION
PER SERVING**
393 calories
38g carbohydrates
19g protein
20g fat
9g fiber

LEVEL UP
Serve this sandwich with a handful of fresh, crunchy vegetables from your Spies Family Crudité (page 47). It's a great way to round out the meal and an easy way to enjoy more veggies in your day!

Spinach, Feta, and Brown Rice Pie

1 tablespoon extra-virgin olive oil

1 onion, finely chopped

3 garlic cloves, minced

10 ounces (283g) frozen spinach, thawed and squeezed of excess water

4 eggs

4 egg whites (about ½ cup)

¼ cup milk (any type will work)

2 cups of Perfectly Cooked Brown Rice (page X)

1 cup feta cheese, broken into large pieces (not crumbs)

¼ teaspoon sea salt

¼ teaspoon pepper

I love any meal that can be made once and enjoyed twice (or more!), especially meals that seem to get better the second time around, like this Spinach, Feta, and Brown Rice Pie. This recipe is similar to a frittata or quiche except it had less egg and more filling! It's perfect as a make-ahead lunch and can of course be enjoyed for a light dinner (or breakfast) as well.

1   Preheat the oven to 425°F (220°C). Coat a 9-inch pie plate with cooking spray or olive oil.

2   Heat oil in a large nonstick skillet over a medium-high heat. Add onion and cook for 3 minutes or until the onions are translucent. Add the garlic and cook for 2 more minutes before stirring in the spinach, salt and pepper. Shut off the heat and cool.

3   In a large bowl, mix together the eggs, egg whites, and milk. Transfer cooled veggie mixture into the bowl, along with the prepared rice and half of the feta cheese. Stir until everything is well combined.

4   Gently pour everything into the prepared pie pan and sprinkle the remaining feta over the top.

5   Bake for 30–40 minutes or until lightly browned and set through. Cool and enjoy.

6   Cover the pie and store in the fridge for up to 5 days.

NUTRITION PER SERVING
237 calories
21g carbohydrates
14g protein
12g fat
3g fiber

LEVEL UP

This is a super flexible dish—think of this recipe as a blueprint and swap in your favorite grains and veggies. This is a great way to use up any leftovers you may have in your fridge.

Whenever I work with feta cheese, I look for feta sold in a block form so I can crumble it myself. Feta sold this way does need any stabilizers or anti-caking agents, so the flavor and texture are superior to pre-crumbled feta cheese.

7 Vegetable Sides

Simply Steamed Artichokes

2 or more large globe
  artichokes

1 tablespoon extra-virgin
  olive oil

½ a lemon

Sea salt and pepper,
  to taste

Artichokes are admittedly one of the most intimidating vegetables you'll encounter, but they are also insanely delicious and well worth learning to make. My family begs me to make this recipe on a weekly basis when artichokes are in season. fresh lemon, melted butter, a vinaigrette, or I often serve them with a shortcut aioli. Combine ¼ cup of your favorite mayonnaise with one fat clove of crushed garlic, a big squeeze of fresh lemon, and a drizzle of extra-virgin olive oil.

1 Trim the bottom of the stems leaving up to 1–inch (2½cm) on each artichoke. Pull off any tough leaves near the bottom of the artichokes.

2 Using a scissors, trim off the thorny ends of each leaf. This will be about ¼–⅓ of the leaf.

3 Grab a sharp knife (I recommend using a serrated knife), and slice off about ¾ to 1-inch (2 to 2½cm) off the top of each artichoke.

4 Rinse the artichokes under cold water. While you rinse them, open the leaves a bit so the water gets inside more easily.

5 In a large pot, add a couple inches of water, the olive oil, and the lemon. Bring the water up to a boil and then reduce it down to a simmer.

6 Place the artichokes, top down, in the bottom of the pot. You should be able to fit 3–4 artichokes depending on the size of your pot. Simmer for 35–45 minutes or until the stems are tender and the thicker bottom leaves pull out easily. Note that you may need to add more water to the pot if levels drop too low, so keep an eye on it.

SERVING

Use tongs to carefully remove the artichokes from the pot. Once they are cool enough to handle, slice them in half lengthwise. Use a spoon to scoop out the choke and any tough leaves near the center (this is not edible so you can toss them).

Serve with garlic aioli, fresh lemon, melted butter, or a vinaigrette.

LEVEL UP:

If you are a visual learner, I have a step-by-step video on YouTube that will walk you though this process. Simply search Dani Spies Artichoke and it will pop right up.

**NUTRITION
PER SERVING**

120 calories

13g carbohydrates

4g protein

7g fat

6g fiber

Popcorn Broccoli

1 large head of broccoli

2 teaspoons extra-virgin olive oil

Fat pinch kosher salt and ground pepper

1 teaspoon garlic powder

1 tablespoon grated Parmesan cheese

Not only is this roasted broccoli recipe nutritious, but it's insanely delicious and as addictive as popcorn according to my husband and kids.

I highly recommend doubling or tripling this recipe because it goes fast! I could easily eat the entire tray all by myself given the chance—it's just that good.

1 Preheat the oven to 400°F (200°C) .

2 Clean and dry the broccoli thoroughly before cutting the florets into bite-sized pieces. It's important that the florets are dry before roasting or they will end up steaming in the oven and you will not get crispy edges. If your broccoli has a stem, don't toss them—use them to make my Dairy-Free Broccoli Stem Soup (page 164).

3 Place all the florets in a large bowl and drizzle with olive oil, salt, pepper, garlic, powder, and Parmesan cheese. Using your hands, toss all the ingredients together, making sure that all the broccoli has a thin coating of the oil and spices.

4 Coat a rimmed baking sheet with cooking spray and place all the broccoli on the sheet. Be sure that the broccoli has space and is not overcrowded. If it seems crowded, use 2 pans.

5 Pop the pan in the oven for 15 minutes, then flip the broccoli and pop back in for another 10 minutes, or until the broccoli is tender on the inside and crispy around the edges.

NUTRITION PER SERVING

117 calories

13g carbohydrates

6g protein

6g fat

5g fiber

LEVEL UP

When shopping for produce, look for local and/or organic products as an easy way to boost the quality of what you are eating. Not only does local and organic produce hold more nutrient density, it often has better flavor as well.

Creamy Crunchy Coleslaw

10-ounce (283g) bag of coleslaw mix or thinly sliced cabbage

1 large garlic clove, crushed

¼ cup nonfat Greek yogurt

¼ cup mayonnaise

¼ cup chopped cilantro or parsley, chopped

¼ teaspoon sea salt

¼ teaspoon pepper

Coleslaw is one of my absolute favorite weeknight sides because it's easy to make, super tasty, and everyone in my family loves it. When I was growing up, my best friend's mom (Mrs. Plaza) made the most delicious coleslaw by keeping things super simple! Her secret? Cabbage and mayonnaise with a good pinch of salt and pepper. I've used this base recipe as my inspiration, except I like to use half mayo and half Greek yogurt. I also add in fresh garlic and herbs for an extra boost of flavor.

1 Combine all the ingredients in a large bowl.

2 Mix until everything is well combined and the cabbage has a light coating of the mayonnaise and Greek yogurt. Adjust seasonings and enjoy.

STORAGE Store in an airtight container in the fridge for up to 3 days.

NUTRITION PER SERVING
122 calories
5g carbohydrates
2g protein
11g fat
2g fiber

LEVEL UP

If you decide to slice your own cabbage, consider adding a shredded carrot as well. It adds a little bit of sweetness and an extra pop of color.

You can easily use all mayonnaise or all Greek yogurt for this recipe, depending on your personal preferences. Both options create a deliciously creamy dressing.

My family loves this recipe served alongside our Oven-Baked Wings (page 231) for a super easy weeknight dinner.

Braised Red Cabbage with Apples and Onions

1 tablespoon
  unsalted butter

1 small onion, thinly sliced

Sea salt and pepper,
  to taste

2 green apples, cored
  and chopped

2 garlic cloves, chopped

1 small head of red
  cabbage (about 2 lbs),
  cored and thinly sliced

¼ cup balsamic vinegar

2 tablespoons honey

¼ cup goat's cheese

2 tablespoons
  chopped parsley

Red cabbage is one of those veggies that is often overlooked and underestimated. While I absolutely love the texture of red cabbage when it's raw and often include it in my salads, this braised red cabbage recipe is sweet, tender and a completely different kind of delicious. I first had braised cabbage at a restaurant called Houston's, and immediately knew I needed to recreate this recipe at home.

1 Melt the butter in a large nonstick saucepan or Dutch oven over medium-high heat.

2 Add the onion along with a pinch of salt and sauté for 6–8 minutes, or until the onion is tender and translucent. If the onion begins to brown, turn down the heat.

3 Add the apples and garlic to the pan. Season with a little more salt and pepper, stir and cook for 2 minutes.

4 Next, stir in the red cabbage, balsamic vinegar, honey and a splash of water. Season again with salt and pepper, and gently stir everything together.

5 Allow the cabbage to slowly simmer on the stove for 30 minutes, stirring every so often. If the pan seems dry, add more water as needed (the water will evaporate as the cabbage cooks).

6 Once the cabbage is tender and buttery, transfer to a serving dish and top with small crumbles of goat's cheese and freshly chopped parsley.

**NUTRITION
PER SERVING**
156 calories
28g carbohydrates
4g protein
4g fat
5g fiber

LEVEL UP
Red cabbage is rich in vitamin C, vitamin K, and is a low-calorie source of dietary fiber! This colorful and tasty veggie helps to support our immune system and our digestive system.

Roasted Brussels Sprouts with Grapes

1 lb Brussels sprouts, trimmed and halved

½ lb seedless red grapes, halved

2 garlic cloves, crushed

1 tablespoon extra-virgin olive oil

½ teaspoon kosher salt

¼ teaspoon pepper

1 tablespoon balsamic glaze

This recipe was originally born when one of my viewers from YouTube requested that I make this dish for Thanksgiving. I had never heard of this combination before and couldn't believe how delicious it was. The sweet and savory combination of the Brussels sprouts and the grapes makes for the most delicious bite!

1 Preheat the oven to 400°F (200°C).

2 Combine the Brussels sprouts, grapes, and garlic in a large bowl. Drizzle with the olive oil and season with salt and pepper. Toss everything together until the Brussels sprouts and grapes are lightly coated.

3 Spread everything out on a rimmed baking sheet and roast for 25–30 minutes, flipping halfway through, or until the Brussels sprouts are golden brown.

4 Transfer to your favorite serving dish and drizzle with balsamic glaze.

NUTRITION PER SERVING

128 calories

23g carbohydrates

4g protein

4g fat

5g fiber

LEVEL UP

While you can easily buy balsamic glaze at the grocery store, it's also super easy to make from scratch. Combine 2 cups balsamic vinegar with ¼ cup honey in a small saucepan and bring to a boil. Reduce the heat and simmer for 10–15 minutes, stirring occasionally, until the vinegar is thick enough to coat the back of a spoon. You can use it immediately or store in the fridge for up to 3 months.

Sautéed Collard Greens with Onions and Raisins

1 tablespoon extra-virgin
olive oil

2 small yellow onions,
thinly sliced

3 garlic cloves, minced

1–2 large bunches collard
greens, sliced

2 tablespoons raisins

Sea salt and pepper,
to taste

Collard greens are a member of the cabbage family; they're a dark leafy green that pack a nutritional punch. While they are often overlooked at the grocery store, I encourage you to pick up a bunch next time you see them. We grow them in our garden and find them easy to work with and delicious. Many people throw away the stems, but if my collards are young and tender, I chop them up and add them to the recipe!

1 To prepare the greens, cut the thick center rib and stem out of each collard leaf. Finely chop the stems and set them aside. Stack the leaves and roll them into a cigar-like shape. Slice this collard cigar into thin ribbons—I try to slice them as thin as possible. Then go back across the other way so the ribbons aren't so long.

2 Heat the olive oil over medium heat in a large nonstick skillet. Add the onions and sauté, stirring often, for about 15 minutes or until onions are golden brown. If the onions begin to burn, turn the heat down.

3 Toss the chopped stems and the garlic into the pan and sauté for another 5 minutes, or until the stems have softened.

4 Add the leafy green ribbons along with $\frac{1}{3}$ cup water to the pan. Season with salt and pepper and cook for about 5 minutes or until the greens have wilted.

5 Toss in the raisins and cook another 2–3 minutes to allow the raisins to warm up. Adjust seasonings and enjoy.

STORAGE Store cooked collard greens in a sealed container in the refrigerator once completely cooled. They will keep for up to 4 days.

**NUTRITION
PER SERVING**
75 calories
16g carbohydrates
4g protein
1g fat
5g fiber

LEVEL UP ──────────────────────
When you add the collards to the skillet it will look like a lot of greens, but don't worry, they will cook down quite a bit.

If you don't have collard greens, this recipe would also work well with Swiss chard, kale, mustard greens or baby spinach. Keep in mind that collards are a little tougher than most greens and will require more cooking time.

If you enjoy heat, a sprinkle of crushed red pepper flakes work really well with the sweetness of the raisins.

Sautéed Broccoli Rabe

1 tablespoon extra-virgin olive oil

3–4 garlic cloves, chopped

¼ teaspoon crushed red pepper flakes

1 bunch broccoli rabe

Sea salt and pepper, to taste

Fresh lemon, for serving

Broccoli rabe, also called rapini, is a cruciferous vegetable closely related to turnips and mustard greens. It has an enjoyably bitter yet nutty flavor that reminds me of when I was a kid. Growing up, both my mom and dad would often make a double-batch of this nutritious green on the weekend to have on hand as an easy side or quick snack during the week.

1 Trim about a ½-inch (1cm) off of the ends of the broccoli rabe.

2 Bring a large pot of salted water to a boil and set up an ice bath by filling a large bowl with cold water and ice.

3 Drop the broccoli rabe into the boiling water and blanch for 2 minutes. Remove using a pair of kitchen tongs and plunge in the ice water to cool, about 30 seconds. Drain and place on a clean kitchen towel to dry off.

4 Heat oil in a large skillet over medium heat. Stir in the garlic and red pepper flakes and cook for about 1 minute or until fragrant. Add the broccoli rabe, salt and pepper and toss in the oil and garlic, cooking for 3–5 minutes or until vibrant and tender.

5 Remove from the pan, being sure not to miss any bits of garlic, drain off excess liquid, adjust seasonings and finish with a squeeze of lemon juice.

NUTRITION PER SERVING

49 calories
3g carbohydrates
2g protein
4g fat
2g fiber

LEVEL UP

If the pan looks dry or the garlic is browning too quickly when cooking your broccoli rabe, add a splash of chicken or vegetable broth to the pan. This is an easy way to add flavor without using an excess of oil.

prep **10 minutes** / cook **40 minutes** / makes **4 servings**

Roasted Spaghetti Squash

1 spaghetti squash (about 4-5 lbs)
1 tablespoon extra-virgin olive oil
1 teaspoon garlic powder
½ teaspoon sea salt
¼ teaspoon pepper
¼ cup Parmesan cheese
Pinch of crushed red pepper flakes

Once it's cooked, spaghetti squash shreds into long strands that visually resemble spaghetti, hence the name. It's delicious with a drizzle of extra-virgin olive oil, salt, pepper and Parmesan cheese, and it also works well as a low-carb, nutrient-dense pasta swap. I love to serve it as the base for Turkey Bolognese (page 186) and my Turkey and Zucchini Skillet (page 222). I also use it as the star of the show in my Spaghetti Squash with Garlicky Greens (page 188).

1 Preheat the oven to 400°F (200°C).

2 Trim each end of the spaghetti squash (this will make it easier to cut in half). Stand the squash on one end and slice in half lengthwise. I find rocking the knife back and forth the best way to get the job done, but be careful.

3 Scoop out the seeds and any stringy ribbing from each half of the squash.

4 Drizzle the inside of the squash with the olive oil and season with the garlic powder, salt, and pepper.

5 Place the halves, cut-side down, on a rimmed baking sheet lined with parchment paper. Roast for 30-40 minutes, or until lightly browned on the outside and fork tender. The time will vary depending on the size of your squash.

6 Remove from the oven and flip the squash so that it is cut side up. When cool enough to handle, use a fork to scrape and fluff the strands from the sides of the squash.

7 Serve topped with red pepper flakes and Parmesan cheese.

NUTRITION PER SERVING
86 calories
17g carbohydrates
2g protein
2g fat
4g fiber

LEVEL UP
Swapping traditional pasta for spaghetti squash is a great way to lighten up a meal while adding more nutrient density.

Perfectly Roasted Sweet Potato Bites

2 large sweet potatoes

1 tablespoon extra-virgin olive oil

1 teaspoon garlic powder

¼ teaspoon sea salt

¼ teaspoon pepper

Roasted sweet potato bites are one of my all-time favorite veggie sides. I first had them when I lived in California, then I decided to recreate them at home. These little gems are crispy and salty on the outside and tender and pillowy on the inside. Serve them as an easy weeknight side, add them to a salad or pair them with some eggs for breakfast.

1 Preheat the oven to 425°F (220°C) and coat a rimmed baking sheet with cooking spray.

2 Scrub your sweet potatoes under cold water. I like to leave the skin on as it holds a lot of nutrients and tastes delicious but if preferred, you can peel the skins.

3 Use a sharp knife to cut the sweet potatoes into hearty bite-sized chunks. I like to trim off the ends of the potato, slice them in half horizontally, lay them flat-side down, then come over the top and slice each half in half vertically—this will leave you with four quarters. Lay each quarter flat-side down, slice lengthwise into three strips, then come back the other way to create chunks.

4 Place sweet potatoes on the prepared baking sheet, drizzle with the olive oil and season with the garlic powder, salt, and pepper.

5 Bake for 15–20 minutes, flip, and cook for another 5–10 minutes or until the potatoes are golden brown on the outside and tender in the middle. Serve and enjoy.

LEVEL UP

Be sure not to overcrowd the pan when roasting your sweet potatoes. This will result in steamed potatoes and you won't get the rich, caramelized color and flavor that make this recipe so good.

You can make this recipe with any type of sweet potatoes—yams, white sweet potatoes, or purple sweet potatoes all work well. Try using a combination of different varieties to create a beautiful and colorful final dish.

Add one teaspoon of curry powder or garam masala when seasoning your potatoes. Both have anti-inflammatory properties and their warm, smoky flavors pair well with the sweet nuttiness of the potatoes.

NUTRITION PER SERVING

180 calories

35g carbohydrates

3g protein

4g fat

5g fiber

8 Soups & Chili

Creamy Asparagus Soup

1 tablespoon extra-virgin
  olive oil

1 medium onion, chopped

Sea salt and pepper,
  to taste

1 garlic clove, chopped

2 lbs asparagus, trimmed
  and cut into 1-inch
  (2.5cm) pieces

1x 15-ounce (425g) can
  cannellini beans, drained
  and rinsed

4 cups low-sodium
  vegetable broth (or
  filtered water)

This rich and creamy asparagus soup uses just 6 ingredients and is thickened with white beans, making it 100% dairy-free. A light, vibrant soup that is also warm and comforting, I love whipping this up when I want something easy and nourishing. While I do prefer to make this recipe with fresh asparagus, you can also make it with frozen asparagus.

1 Heat the olive oil in a large pot, add the onion with a pinch of salt. Sauté the onion until it is translucent and tender (not browned); this takes about 5 minutes.

2 Add in the garlic, asparagus, and beans. Season with a bit of salt and pepper and give it all a stir. Pour in the broth, turn the heat to high and bring to a boil.

3 Reduce the heat to a simmer and cook for 5-10 minutes, or until the asparagus is fork tender (the time will vary depending on the thickness of your asparagus). Shut off the heat and let the soup cool for a few minutes before blending.

4 Working in batches, spoon the soup into your blender, filling the blender no more than a quarter to a third of the way up. Place the lid on, leaving it slightly ajar so steam can escape, and blend until the soup is rich and creamy. Repeat until you have finished all the soup and then return the soup to the pot to warm.

5 Alternatively, you can use an immersion blender and blend the soup directly in the pot.

6 Serve topped with an extra crack of black pepper and enjoy.

STORAGE This soup will last up to 5 days in your fridge when stored in an airtight container. If you want to freeze this soup, let it cool completely and then transfer into an airtight, freezer-safe container. This soup will last in your freezer for up to 3 months.

**NUTRITION
PER SERVING**
177 calories
31g carbohydrates
11g protein
4g fat
10g fiber

LEVEL UP

I love to drizzle a bit of coconut milk (or you can sub half-and-half) over the top as it adds an extra layer of creaminess and looks absolutely beautiful.

Try adding a sprinkle of protein-packed hemp seeds! Their flavor pairs well with the asparagus and the added fat and protein can help you feel satiated for longer.

Green Detox Soup

1 tablespoon coconut oil
  or extra-virgin olive oil

1 medium onion, chopped

6 garlic cloves, peeled
  and roughly chopped

1 tablespoon
  grated ginger

Sea salt, to taste

2 medium
  zucchini, chopped

4 cups Kale Ribbons
  (page 48)

4 cups broccoli florets

4 cups low-sodium
  vegetable broth

1 cup chopped parsley

1 cup chopped cilantro

Inspired by my friend Helene, I love to have this rich, flavorful, nutrient-dense soup on hand to sip throughout the colder months. I intentionally make a big batch of this soup and store it in jars in my fridge, so I have it ready to grab-n-go throughout the week. It also freezes really well!

1 Melt the oil in a large pot or Dutch oven over medium heat. Add the onion, garlic, ginger, and a pinch of salt and cook until the onion is translucent and fragrant; about 5 minutes.

2 Add in the zucchini, kale, broccoli, broth, and 2 cups of water. The liquid should be about even with the vegetables, don't worry if some of the veggies are popping out. Bring everything to a boil and then reduce to a simmer, partially cover and cook for 10 minutes or until the broccoli is tender.

3 Turn off the heat, pop the lid back on and let the soup sit until it is cool enough to handle.

4 Working in batches, add the soup to a blender with a small handful of the parsley, cilantro, and little pinch of salt in each batch. Be careful not to fill the blender more than halfway and then blend until rich and creamy. If the soup seems too thick, add a bit of water until you have your desired consistency.

5 Transfer the soup into jars and repeat until you have blended all the soup.

STORAGE This soup will last up to 5 days stored in an airtight container in your fridge and up to 3 months in the freezer.

**NUTRITION
PER SERVING**
58 calories
9.8g carbohydrates
3.1g protein
1.7g fat
2.4g fiber

LEVEL UP

When serving this soup in a bowl, I love to add a swirl of coconut milk to the top.

Add a bit of plant-based protein and healthy fat to this soup by topping it with 1–2 tablespoons of hemp seeds. They have a really mild, slightly nutty flavor and creamy texture while being rich in protein and heart-healthy, omega-3 fatty acids.

Dairy-Free Broccoli Stem Soup

Stems from one large
head of broccoli

1 tablespoon extra-virgin
olive oil

½ medium onion, sliced

2 garlic cloves, chopped

¼ teaspoon sea salt

¼ teaspoon pepper

2-3 cups low-sodium
chicken broth

If you have ever found yourself making a recipe that calls for broccoli florets but you didn't know what to do with the stems, this recipe is for you! This is a light and refreshing soup that comes together in less than 30 minutes and can be enjoyed anytime of the year.

1 Trim any fibrous bits from the broccoli stems and then slice them into thin coins. You should end up with 4–5 cups of broccoli coins from one large head of broccoli.

2 Heat the olive oil in a medium pot and stir in the onion, garlic, and broccoli stems. Season the veggies with half of the salt and pepper and allow to cook for about 10 minutes. Stir periodically until the veggies are tender and the onions are translucent.

3 Pour the chicken broth into the pot—start with 2 cups and then add the remaining cup if you prefer a thinner soup. Simmer for 5 minutes and then shut off the heat.

4 Remove the pot from the stove and allow the soup to cool for a few minutes before pouring into a high-speed blender. Be sure not to fill your blender more than halfway and leave the lid slightly ajar so the heat has room to escape.

5 Blend for 15–20 seconds, or until thick and creamy. If needed, add more broth to reach your preferred texture and season with remaining salt and pepper.

6 Serve with an extra drizzle of olive oil and some cracked pepper.

STORAGE Store cooled, leftover soup in an airtight container in the fridge for up to 4 days.

**NUTRITION
PER SERVING**

62 calories

3g carbohydrates

4g protein

1g fat

5g fiber

LEVEL UP ─────────

If you want to keep this recipe 100% plant-based, simply replace the chicken broth with veggie broth or water.

Have extra greens in your fridge that you don't want to go to waste? Sauté them with your broccoli stems to add more nutrients to this soup while avoiding any extra waste!

Escarole and Beans

1 tablespoon extra-virgin
  olive oil

6 garlic cloves, chopped

Pinch of crushed red
  pepper flakes

1 lb escarole, washed and
  chopped (2 small-
  medium bunches)

3 cups low-sodium
  chicken broth

½ teaspoon dried oregano

1x 15-ounce (425g) can
  cannellini beans

Sea salt and pepper,
  to taste

Parmesan cheese,
  for topping

Escarole and beans (aka scarola e fagioli) is a simple, comforting, classic Italian dish that I grew up eating. It's an easy, nourishing meal that comes together quickly and will warm your soul from the inside out. I love to serve this topped with Parmesan cheese and red pepper flakes along with some crusty sourdough bread on the side. If you want to keep this meal 100% plant-based, sub in vegetable broth for the chicken broth.

1 Heat the olive oil in a large pot or Dutch oven over medium heat. Add in garlic and red pepper flakes and sauté until fragrant.

2 Toss in the escarole along with ½ cup of broth, oregano, and a pinch of salt and pepper. Stir well, pop on a lid and simmer for 5 minutes.

3 Remove the lid, pour in the beans and the liquid from the can along with the remaining chicken broth. Simmer for another 10–15 minutes, or until the greens have wilted down and are tender.

4 Ladle into your favorite bowl and top with freshly grated Parmesan cheese, red pepper flakes, and a drizzle of olive oil.

**NUTRITION
PER SERVING**
94 calories
9g carbohydrates
6g protein
5g fat
4g fiber

LEVEL UP
Escarole is a pleasantly bitter, leafy green that is rich in fiber, Vitamin A, Vitamin C, and antioxidants. It looks a lot like a head of lettuce but with thicker, broader leaves and is closely related to endive and frisée, as all are members of the chicory family.

Escarole can also be enjoyed in my Italian Wedding Soup (page 172) and is also delicious enjoyed raw in salads.

Best Black Bean Soup

1 tablespoon extra-virgin olive oil

1 large onion, chopped

Sea salt and pepper, to taste

3 bell peppers, chopped

6 garlic cloves, chopped

1 tablespoon cumin

1 teaspoon chili powder

1 teaspoon dried oregano

4x 15-ounce (425g) cans black beans, rinsed and drained

4 cups low-sodium chicken broth

1 tablespoon fresh lime juice

Optional toppings: sliced scallions, diced avocado, cilantro, diced radishes, tortilla chips

My husband and I met working in a Mexican restaurant and before each shift, we were able to choose a meal to enjoy. Black bean soup was one of my personal favorites, so I love recreating this memory at home. This is a delicious, nourishing, soup that is loaded with fiber, which can help us feel satiated for longer periods of time. Using canned black beans helps to keep this soup easy enough to make for dinner any night of the week. Be sure to add your favorite toppings to really elevate this dish.

1 Heat the olive oil in a large pot over a medium heat. Add the onions along with a pinch of salt and cook, stirring periodically, for 5 minutes, or until the onions are just beginning to look translucent.

2 Stir in the bell peppers, garlic, cumin, chili powder, oregano, salt and pepper. Cook for about 5 minutes or until the peppers have softened and veggies are fragrant.

3 Pour in black beans and broth and bring up to a boil and then reduce to a gentle simmer and cook for 20–30 minutes, or until the broth is flavorful.

4 Scoop half of the soup into a blender (about 4 cups) and blend until smooth. Be careful not to fill your blender more than halfway and leave the lid slightly ajar. Start blending on low, allowing steam to escape from the blender.

5 Return the blended soup to the pot and a squeeze of fresh lime juice and adjust the seasonings. Serve with your favorite toppings and enjoy!

STORAGE This soup will last in the fridge for up to 5 days when stored in an airtight container and for up to 3 months in the freezer.

NUTRITION PER SERVING
307 calories
27g carbohydrates
6g protein
21g fat
10g fiber

LEVEL UP

If you want to keep this recipe 100% plant-based, sub out the chicken broth for some low-sodium vegetable broth instead.

My family loves this soup, we serve it with homemade Guacamole (page X) and corn chips on the side.

After blending, sneak some extra greens into your meal by adding in some Kale Ribbons (page 48) or chopped baby spinach before serving.

Hearty Minestrone Soup

1 lb Italian chicken
sausage, casings
removed

1 tablespoon olive oil, plus
an extra teaspoon for
the pasta

1 small onion, chopped

2-3 celery stalks, chopped

2-3 carrots, chopped

1 teaspoon sea salt

2 garlic cloves, chopped

1 teaspoon dried oregano

1 teaspoon
poultry seasoning

½ teaspoon pepper

4 cups thinly
sliced cabbage

1 large zucchini, chopped

1x 28-ounce (793g) can
diced tomatoes

4 cups low-sodium
chicken stock

12 ounces (340g) brown
rice elbow pasta

1¼ cups canned cannellini
beans, drained
and rinsed

2 cups baby
spinach, chopped

⅓ cup chopped basil
or parsley

Fat pinch of crushed red
pepper flakes (optional)

2 tablespoons Parmesan
cheese (optional)

Minestrone is an Italian soup that was traditionally made to use up leftover vegetables, so use what you have on hand. I recommend cooking the pasta separately and adding it to the bottom of the bowl before serving, as this will prevent it from getting mushy. If you prefer a lower carb minestrone, skip the pasta and add a couple extra cups of vegetables. Or swap out the chicken broth for veggie, if you prefer. As always, use this recipe as a blueprint and make it work for you!

1 Heat a heavy 6-quart pot over medium heat and add the sausage to the pot, breaking it up until you have small crumbles. Cook for 10 minutes, or until lightly browned and cooked through—the meat will turn from translucent to opaque. Remove from the pan and set aside. Drain any excess fat from the pan.

2 Add the olive oil to the pot along with the onion, celery, carrots, and half of the salt. Stir and cook for 8–10 minutes or until veggies are tender and fragrant.

3 Add in garlic and stir. Cook for 1 minute before adding in the spices: oregano, poultry seasoning, remaining salt, and pepper. Stir well.

4 Next, add in the cabbage, zucchini, diced tomatoes, and chicken stock. Stir to combine and bring everything to a boil. Reduce heat to a simmer, partially covered, for 20 minutes.

5 In the meantime, cook the pasta according to package directions. Drain, return to the pot, and drizzle with olive oil so it doesn't stick.

6 Stir in the cannellini beans, baby spinach, fresh parsley, and the cooked sausage. Cook until the greens are wilted down and beans are heated through.

7 If your soup needs to be thinned out a bit, stir in some extra broth.

8 Scoop pasta into the bottom of your bowl, ladle soup over the top and serve topped with grated Parmesan cheese and red chili flakes.

STORAGE Stored in an airtight container, this soup will last in your fridge for up to 5 days and in the freezer for up to 3 months. Be sure to store the pasta in a separate container so it does not become mushy.

**NUTRITION
PER SERVING**
437 calories
51g carbohydrates
24g protein
18g fat
9g fiber

Italian Wedding Soup

For the meatballs

1 lb ground turkey

1 small onion, diced

2 garlic cloves, crushed

⅓ cup finely
   chopped parsley

¼ cup Parmesan cheese

¼ cup whole wheat
   panko breadcrumbs

1 large egg

½ teaspoon sea salt

½ teaspoon pepper

For the soup

12 cups low-sodium
   chicken broth

1 lb escarole, washed and
   roughly chopped

2 large eggs

2 tablespoons Parmesan
   cheese, plus more
   for serving

Pepper, for serving

Warm and comforting, this soup cooks in under an hour but tastes like it's slow cooked on the stovetop all day. Loaded with tiny turkey meatballs and lots of vegetables, this is healthy, family-friendly comfort food at its best. I love to use escarole as the greens for this soup, but curly endive, kale, and spinach would also work well.

1   In a large bowl, combine all of the meatball ingredients. Use your hands to combine everything together and then free-form little meatballs, resting them on a rimmed baking sheet as you work. I use about a tablespoon per meatball and end up with roughly 40 meatballs. If the meat mixture feels sticky, keep a small bowl of cold water nearby and keep your hands damp—this will make rolling the meatballs easier.

2   Add the chicken broth to a large pot and bring to a boil over a medium-high heat. Gently add the meatballs into the soup followed by the escarole. Cook for 10 minutes or until the greens are wilted and the meatballs are cooked through (you will notice the meatballs will begin to float to the top as they cook).

3   In a small bowl, whisk together the eggs and Parmesan cheese and then gently drizzle into the soup, stirring the soup as you pour. You will end up with thin strands of egg throughout your soup.

4   Serve with an extra sprinkle of Parmesan cheese and black pepper over the top. If you like a bit of extra spice, add a sprinkle of crushed red pepper flakes.

STORAGE   This soup can be stored in an airtight container in the refrigerator for up to 5 days or in the freezer for up to 3 months.

**NUTRITION
PER SERVING**

248 calories

13g carbohydrates

34g protein

8g fat

3g fiber

LEVEL UP:
I love to make this recipe with ground turkey, but you can swap in ground chicken or beef as well.

If you want to sneak another vegetable into this recipe (or if you are gluten-free), try swapping the breadcrumbs for steamed cauliflower rice.

Creamy Chicken and Wild Rice Soup

½ cup wild rice

1 tablespoon extra-virgin olive oil

1 small onion, chopped

3–4 carrots, chopped

3 large celery stalks, chopped

Sea salt, to taste

2 garlic cloves, finely chopped

8 ounces (226g) cremini mushrooms, finely chopped

8–10 cups low-sodium chicken broth

1 tablespoon low-sodium soy sauce (use Tamari for a gluten-free option)

1 bay leaf

½ cup canned coconut milk

2 heaping cups shredded Baked Bone-In Chicken Breasts (page 54)

4 cups Kale Ribbons (page 48)

Pepper, to taste

This is a creamy, hearty soup that is thickened with coconut milk and packed with bits of shredded chicken, nutty wild rice and plenty of veggies! I always bake the chicken ahead of time (page 54) to keep this recipe super easy. If you don't have time to bake your own chicken, rotisserie is a fantastic shortcut. My family loves this soup as a cold-weather Sunday dinner served with some sourdough bread from our favorite local bakery.

1 Rinse the wild rice under cold water and set aside.

2 Heat the olive oil in a large Dutch oven over medium-high heat. Add in the onion, carrots, celery and a pinch of salt. Sauté for 10 minutes, or until the veggies are fragrant and the onions are translucent.

3 Stir in the garlic and mushrooms, cook for another 5 minutes. Once the veggies are just tender, add in the wild rice, chicken broth, soy sauce, and bay leaf. Turn the heat to high and bring everything up to a boil, then reduce down to a simmer and cook, partially covered, for about 40 minutes, or until the wild rice is tender.

4 Stir in the coconut milk, chicken, and kale ribbons, and season to taste with salt and pepper.

5 Simmer for another 5–10 minutes, or until the kale has wilted (but is still vibrant). Remove the bay leaf and enjoy!

STORAGE This soup is perfect for meal prep because the flavors seem to get even better over time! Make a big pot on the weekend and then store in an airtight container in your fridge for up to 5 days.

LEVEL UP

Start with 8 cups of broth and only add the extra broth if you want the soup to be thinner (this will be a personal preference). If you want the soup to be even creamier, use the entire can of coconut milk and pull back on the broth just a bit.

Wild rice is a healthy grain option that has fewer calories and more protein than brown rice. It's also gluten free and loaded with antioxidants like zinc, magnesium and phosphorus. It has a delicious chewy, earthy flavor and is super easy to make.

NUTRITION PER SERVING
358 calories
31g carbohydrates
14g protein
14g fat
2g fiber

Turkey Butternut Squash Chili

1 tablespoon extra-virgin
  olive oil

1 medium yellow
  onion, chopped

1 bell pepper, chopped

4 garlic cloves,
  finely chopped

2 lbs ground turkey

1 butternut squash,
  peeled, seeded and cut
  into ½-inch (1cm) cubes

1 tablespoon chili powder

2 teaspoons cumin

1 teaspoon cinnamon

2 teaspoons
  smoked paprika

1 teaspoon sea salt

½ teaspoon pepper

1x 28-ounce (793g) can
  diced fire roasted
  tomatoes

4 cups low-sodium
  chicken broth

1x 15-ounce (425g) can
  black beans, rinsed
  and drained

1x 15-ounce (425g) can
  chickpeas, rinsed
  and drained

A few big handfuls of
  baby spinach, chopped

Greek yogurt and fresh
  sliced scallions, to
  top (optional)

This delicious, hearty chili recipe is healthy comfort food at its best. Warm, cozy spices paired with ground turkey, beans and butternut squash taste like a hug in a bowl. You may not even notice that you are enjoying a nutrient-dense meal packed with protein and veggies, but your body sure will! Make a big pot on the weekend and have it ready to go for a busy week. Or better yet, save it for a quiet Sunday night and enjoy it with the people you love most!

1 Heat the olive oil in a large pot or Dutch oven over medium heat. Add in the onion, pepper and garlic along with a pinch of salt. Cook for 6–8 minutes or until the veggies have softened and the onions are translucent.

2 Push the veggies to the side and add in the ground turkey. Break the turkey up with a wooden spoon until it is in small crumbles and cook until the turkey is no longer pink in the middle.

3 Add in the butternut squash, chili powder, cumin, cinnamon, smoked paprika, salt and pepper. Give everything a big stir and then add in the tomatoes and chicken broth. Turn up the heat and bring everything up to a boil. Reduce the heat, add in the beans, and chickpeas, and simmer for 30 minutes.

4 Once the squash is tender and all the flavors have come together, stir in the chopped spinach, cook until wilted and then serve and enjoy topped with yogurt and scallions, if you desire.

**NUTRITION
PER SERVING**
336 calories
30g carbohydrates
42g protein
7g fat
6g fiber

LEVEL UP

If you want a step-by-step guide on how to cut a butternut squash, be sure to watch the YouTube video that accompanies this recipe.

You can also take a shortcut and buy pre-peeled and cut butternut squash at the grocery store. This will cost a little more money but it will save you a lot of time.

Best Beef Chili

1 tablespoon olive oil

1 medium yellow onion, chopped

1 green bell pepper, chopped

4 garlic cloves, chopped

½ teaspoon sea salt

1 tablespoon chili powder

1 teaspoon dried oregano

1 tablespoon tomato paste

1 chipotle pepper in adobo, coarsely chopped with 1 tablespoon sauce

1 lb grass-fed ground beef

1x 15-ounce (425g) can low-sodium chicken broth

1x 15-ounce (425g) can diced tomatoes

1x 15-ounce (425g) can kidney beans, rinsed and drained

1x 15-ounce (425g) can pinto beans, rinsed and drained

Shredded cheese, scallions, Greek yogurt, and/or Guacamole (page 90), for serving (optional)

Delicious, healthy and hearty, this classic chili is made with grass-fed ground beef, two types of beans, veggies, tomatoes and warm spices. This is an easy one-pot meal that is high in fiber and protein, comes together quickly and is perfect for meal prep.

1 Heat the olive oil in a large pot or Dutch oven over medium-high heat. Add the onion, pepper, garlic, salt, chili powder, and oregano. Cook for about 3–5 minutes or until the veggies are fragrant and beginning to soften.

2 Stir in the tomato paste, chipotle chili and sauce; cook for another minute before adding the ground beef, breaking it up with a wooden spoon, and cook until the meat is browned (about 5 minutes).

3 Add the broth and simmer for about 10 minutes. Stir in the tomatoes and the beans; bring to a boil. Cook, uncovered, stirring occasionally until thick (about 10 minutes).

4 Ladle chili into bowls and top with your favorite toppings.

STORAGE This chili will keep in your fridge for up to 5 days. Once your chili is completely cooled, place it in an airtight container (or multiple, if you'd like to meal prep it) without any additional toppings and place it in the fridge. To reheat it, simply pop it in the microwave using a microwave-safe bowl, or you can reheat it on the stovetop.

To freeze, place chili into airtight freezer-safe containers. Freeze for up to 3 months. Remember to label the chili with the date, so you remember when you placed it into the freezer. When you're ready to enjoy the chili, thaw it in the refrigerator overnight, then reheat it on the stovetop or microwave until it is warmed through.

NUTRITION PER SERVING
365 calories
39g carbohydrates
28g protein
11g fat
13g fiber

LEVEL UP
The secret ingredient in this recipe are the chipotle peppers in adobo sauce. Adobo sauce is a dark red chile sauce made from ground dried chiles that are smoked and cooked with tangy tomatoes and spices. It has a warm, smokey, flavor and add a lot of depth without adding extra cooking time.

Make an easy sauce by combining 1 tablespoon of adobo sauce with ¼ cup Greek yogurt to use on sandwiches, tacos, quesadillas, and scrambled eggs.

Vegetarian Sweet Potato Chili

1 tablespoon olive oil

1 medium red onion, chopped

1 green bell pepper, chopped

1 yellow bell pepper, chopped

2 medium sweet potatoes, peeled and chopped

4 garlic cloves, chopped

1 tablespoon chili powder

2 teaspoons cumin

2 teaspoons curry powder

Sea salt and pepper, to taste

1x 28-ounce (793g) can fire roasted diced tomatoes

1x 15-ounce (425g) can black beans, drained and rinsed

1x 15-ounce (425g) can chickpeas, drained and rinsed

4 cups low-sodium vegetable broth

Juice of one lime

¼ cup chopped cilantro

Shredded cheddar cheese, Greek yogurt, chopped onions or radishes and/or homemade Guacamole (page 90), for serving (optional)

This plant-based veggie chili is hearty and delicious enough to convert any meat lover in your home. Loaded with sweet potatoes, black beans, chickpeas and lots of warm, cozy spices, this is a super-satisfying meal that won't leave anyone "missing the meat." I always top this chili with my homemade Guacamole (page 90), it's the perfect combination.

1 Heat the olive oil in a 5-quart pot over medium-high heat. Add in the onions, peppers, and sweet potatoes along with a pinch of salt. Cook, stirring occasionally, until the onions begin to turn translucent and everything is fragrant, about 5 minutes.

2 Stir in the garlic, chili powder, cumin, and curry powder along with a little more salt and some black pepper. Add the tomatoes, beans, and broth and stir.

3 Bring everything up to a light boil and then reduce to a simmer. Cook for 20–30 minutes, stirring occasionally, or until the potatoes are tender and the chili has reduced and has a nice hearty consistency. Serve in your favorite bowl and top with your favorite chili toppings.

NUTRITION PER SERVING

270 calories

49g carbohydrates

10g protein

5g fat

12g fiber

LEVEL UP

Add an extra boost of nutrition to this delicious chili by stirring in a big handful of Kale Ribbons (page 48) or some chopped baby spinach.

9 Pasta & Grains

KK's Pantry Puttanesca

1 tablespoon extra-virgin
  olive oil

3 garlic cloves,
  finely chopped

4 anchovy filets, chopped

½ teaspoon crushed red
  pepper flakes

Sea salt and pepper,
  to taste

1x 28-ounce (793g) can
  diced tomatoes

1 teaspoon dried oregano

¾ cup pitted Kalamata
  olives, halved

3 tablespoons capers,
  drained

¼ cup chopped basil
  (parsley also works)

8 ounces (226g) dried
  brown rice spaghetti
  (or whatever pasta
  you love)

1 lb zucchini noodles
  (from 2 large zucchini)

2 tablespoons Parmesan
  cheese

After trying puttanesca sauce at a restaurant near the beach, my daughter, Katie, quickly requested that we remake it at home. I love that most of the ingredients come from our pantry, making it an easy option for a busy weeknight dinner. I sneak some extra veggies in by subbing half of the pasta with zucchini noodles—such an easy way to level up this meal!

1 Heat the olive oil over medium-low heat in a large nonstick skillet. Add the garlic, anchovies, red pepper flakes, and a small pinch of salt. Cook until fragrant.

2 Add the tomatoes, oregano, olives, and capers. Turn up the heat and simmer for 10 minutes to let all the flavors come together.

3 Finish with salt, pepper, and fresh basil.

4 Meanwhile, cook the pasta in a large pot of boiling salted water until just al dente, according to the package instructions. Add in the zucchini noodles and cook for 2 more minutes, or until the pasta and the zucchini are tender.

5 Drain and add sauce, tossing until coated. Sprinkle with Parmesan cheese, and enjoy!

**NUTRITION
PER SERVING**
347 calories
58g carbohydrates
10g protein
10g fat
8g fiber

LEVEL UP

You can find zucchini noodles in the produce section of many grocery stores. They can also be bought frozen, or you can make them yourself by using a spiralizer. If you want a low-carb meal, you can eliminate the pasta and use all zucchini noodles.

I love the taste and texture of brown rice pasta, it's a gluten-free option that is very family-friendly. But, feel free to use whatever pasta you prefer.

If you want to add some extra protein to this meal, you can stir a can of tuna right into the sauce.

Creamy Butternut Squash Pasta

1 medium butternut squash, peeled and cut into 2-inch (5cm) cubes

1 medium onion, cut into bite-sized chunks

4 garlic cloves, peeled

1 tablespoon extra-virgin olive oil

Sea salt and pepper, to taste

1 lb bucatini pasta

1 cup chicken bone broth

½ cup plain 2% Greek yogurt

½ teaspoon ground sage

Pinch of grated nutmeg

⅓ cup Parmesan cheese

1–2 tablespoons chopped thyme, parsley or basil

½ teaspoon crushed red pepper flakes

Creamy, cozy, and comforting, this simple pasta dish is rich in flavor and easy enough for a weeknight meal. Butternut squash is roasted with onions and garlic before being blended with Greek yogurt, chicken bone broth, and Parmesan cheese to create a dreamy, luxurious sauce. I love to make this dish with a traditional bucatini pasta, but you can sub in any pasta you prefer.

1 Place the butternut squash, onions, and garlic on a rimmed baking sheet, drizzle with olive oil and season with salt and pepper. Transfer into a 425° (220°C) oven and roast for 25–30 minutes, until the squash is tender.

2 While the butternut squash is roasting, cook the pasta until al dente according to package instructions. Drain, reserving a ½ cup of the cooking liquid.

3 When the squash is cool enough to handle, transfer the squash, onions and garlic to a high-speed blender and add the yogurt, bone broth, reserved cooking water, ground sage, and nutmeg.

4 Blend until smooth. Taste and adjust seasoning as needed. Pour 2 cups of the sauce over the pasta (you will have extra sauce), add in Parmesan cheese and toss to coat.

5 Finish with fresh herbs, red pepper flakes, and an extra sprinkle of Parmesan cheese.

STORAGE This recipe makes enough sauce for 2 lbs of pasta. You can keep the leftover pasta sauce in an airtight container in your fridge for up to 5 days and in the freezer for up to 3 months. Simply transfer to a pot when ready to warm or defrost and toss with pasta for a super-quick weeknight meal.

NUTRITION PER SERVING
396 calories
71g carbohydrates
16g protein
2g fat
5g fiber

LEVEL UP

While I recommend that most of your carbohydrate choices be in the form of less refined, less processed foods, I do enjoy traditional pastas on occasion. Cooking pasta al dente will help lower the glycemic load and minimize its effect on blood sugar.

I love to use bone broth for this recipe as one cup adds 10g of protein to this meal. If you can't find bone broth, swap in chicken stock.

Turkey Bolognese over Lentil Penne

1 tablespoon extra-virgin olive oil

1 small onion, finely chopped

1 large carrot, finely chopped

1 celery stalk, finely chopped

2 garlic cloves, diced

Pinch of sea salt, plus more, to taste

1 lb lean ground turkey

2 teaspoons smoked paprika

1 tablespoon Italian seasoning

Pinch of black pepper

1x 28-ounce (793g) can crushed tomatoes

½ cup low-sodium chicken broth

12 ounces (340g) brown rice lentil penne pasta

2 tablespoons half-and-half

2 tablespoons Parmesan cheese

¼ cup chopped basil or parsley

Crushed red pepper flakes, for serving (optional)

Turkey Bolognese is an easy and healthy pasta recipe that is packed with protein and vegetables. This rich, thick sauce tastes like it's been simmering all day, but is ready for dinner in just over 30 minutes. This sauce also works well for meal prep as the flavors get better over time.

1 Heat the oil in a large nonstick skillet or cast-iron pan over medium-high heat. Add in the onion, carrot, celery, garlic, and a pinch of salt. Cook for 8–10 minutes, or until the veggies are tender.

2 Push the veggies to one side of the pan and add in the ground turkey and season with smoked paprika, Italian seasoning, a bit more salt, and a pinch of black pepper. Stir well, mixing the meat, veggies, and seasonings together while breaking the meat into crumbles. Cook unit the turkey is opaque.

3 Pour the crushed tomatoes and chicken broth over the meat and veggie mixture and stir until combined. Simmer over low heat for 15 minutes to allow all of the flavors to come together as the sauce thickens up.

4 Meanwhile, cook the lentil pasta in a large pot of salted, boiling water according to the package instructions. Drain and set aside.

5 Finish the sauce by stirring in the half-and-half, Parmesan cheese, and topping with fresh basil and red pepper flakes (if using). Plate pasta and spoon with sauce over the top. Serve with extra cheese, if desired.

STORAGE When stored in an airtight container, bolognese sauce will last in the fridge for up to 5 days and in the freezer for up to 3 months. If you plan to freeze the sauce, refrain from adding the half-and-half and cheese and add it in when you plan to reheat and serve.

NUTRITION PER SERVING
390 calories
56g carbohydrates
30g protein
7.5g fat
6g fiber

LEVEL UP
Lentil pasta is a great alternative to wheat pasta, with more protein and fiber per serving. You can also swap in zoodles or squash (page 154).

Spaghetti Squash with Garlicky Greens

1 tablespoon extra-virgin
olive oil

2 garlic cloves,
finely chopped

½ medium onion,
chopped

1 bunch collard greens,
stemmed

1 cup low-sodium
chicken broth

5 cups cooked Spaghetti
Squash (page 154)

¼ cup Parmesan cheese

Pinch of crushed red
pepper flakes

Sea salt and pepper,
to taste

Simple and addictive, this recipe is an easy, low carb, pasta-like meal that is a true crowd-pleaser. This dish is hearty enough for a main meal and can also be enjoyed alongside your favorite protein. My kids love this with extra Parmesan cheese and my hubby always adds extra pepper flakes. This dish is a serious nutritional powerhouse, packed with flavor!

1 Wash the greens and stems. Slice stems into small pieces (if they're really thick and tough you can toss them, but if they are young and small they are delicious).

2 Pile the collard leaves on top of one and other, roll into a cigar-like shape, and slice into thin ribbons.

3 Heat the olive oil in a large nonstick skillet. Add the onion, garlic, and collard stems along with a pinch of salt. Cook for 6–8 minutes, or until your veggies are fragrant and beginning to become tender.

4 Add in the collard ribbons, a bit more salt, pepper, and a pinch of red pepper flakes along with chicken broth.

5 Cook for 10–12 minutes or until your greens are nice and tender. Toss in the cooked spaghetti squash and combine everything.

6 Adjust seasonings and top with fresh Parmesan cheese.

STORAGE Store any leftovers in a sealed container in the refrigerator for up to 4 days.

**NUTRITION
PER SERVING**
117 calories
11g carbohydrates
6g protein
6g fat
3g fiber

LEVEL UP

If you don't have collard greens on hand, you can easily sub in some Swiss chard, baby spinach or Kale Ribbons (page 48).

Boost the protein content of this dish by leaning on the C&D Basics and adding in some shredded Simply Poached Salmon (page 58), shredded Baked Bone-in Chicken Breast (page 54) or Crispy Baked Tofu (page 57).

Easy Peanut Soba Noodles

8 ounces (226g)
soba noodles

1 cup shelled edamame

1 red pepper, sliced into
thin strips

2 scallions, thinly sliced

¼ cup chopped cilantro

¼ cup all-natural
peanut butter

2 tablespoons lime juice

2 tablespoons rice vinegar

2 tablespoons low-sodium
soy sauce

1 tablespoon honey

1 tablespoon toasted
sesame oil

1 teaspoon grated ginger

1 clove garlic, crushed

Toasted sesame seeds,
for topping

Crushed red pepper
flakes, fortopping
(optional)

Soba noodles are 100% buckwheat noodles that are naturally gluten-free and rich in fiber. They have a mild flavor and firm texture, making them the perfect base for this easy, flavorful dish. This meal is perfect for a busy weeknight and also works really well packed in lunch boxes.

1 Cook the noodles according to the package instructions. Drain, rinse under cold water, and place in a large bowl topped with the edamame, red pepper, scallions, and cilantro.

2 In a large bowl, whisk together the peanut butter, lime juice, rice vinegar, soy sauce, honey, sesame oil, ginger, and garlic.

3 Pour the peanut sauce over the noodles and toss until everything is lightly coated.

4 Top with sesame seeds and red pepper flakes (if using).

**NUTRITION
PER SERVING**
281 calories
56g carbohydrates
13g protein
3g fat
3g fiber

LEVEL UP
Add an extra boost of protein to this meal by stirring in one cup of shredded Baked Bone-In Chicken Breast (page 54), Simply Poached Salmon (page 58), or Crispy Baked Tofu (page 57).

Brown Rice Power Bowl

For the Peanut Sauce
¼ cup peanut butter
2 tablespoons light
   soy sauce
1 tablespoon maple syrup
2 teaspoons chili
   garlic sauce
2 teaspoons lime juice
1 clove garlic, crushed
1 teaspoon grated ginger
3–4 tablespoons water

For the Power Bowl
2 cups Perfectly Cooked
   Brown Rice (page 51)
1 batch Crispy Baked Tofu
   (page 57)
2 cups broccoli florets
1 cup shelled edamame
1 large carrot, peeled and
   cut into thin rounds
1 cup red cabbage,
   thinly sliced
2 teaspoons black
   sesame seeds

Packed with rice, veggies and crispy baked tofu, this tasty power bowl is drizzled with a creamy peanut sauce and finished with toasted sesame seeds. Prep all of your ingredients in advance to create a simple and nutritious lunch or dinner during the week.

1 Combine peanut butter, soy sauce, maple syrup, chili garlic sauce, lime juice, garlic, and ginger in a small bowl. Whisk with a fork until well combined and creamy. Slowly add water until you have a creamy sauce that is thin enough to drizzle. Set aside.

2 Place a couple inches of water in a saucepan with a steamer basket and bring to a boil. If you don't have a steamer basket, you can put the broccoli directly into the boiling water.

3 Add the broccoli to the steamer and cover. Reduce the heat to a simmer and cook for 4–6 minutes, or until the broccoli is tender and vibrant. Remove and set aside.

4 To build your bowl, divide all of the ingredients amongst 4 bowls: prepared brown rice, crispy tofu, broccoli florets, edamame, carrot slices, and shredded cabbage.

5 Drizzle the peanut sauce over the top of each bowl and finish with a sprinkle of sesame seeds.

**NUTRITION
PER SERVING**
405 calories
23g carbohydrates
21g protein
16g fat
5.4g fiber

LEVEL UP —————————————————————
This is a super versatile recipe. Change up the protein by swapping the tofu with shredded Baked Bone-in Chicken Breast (page 54) or Simply Poached Salmon (page 58) or swap out the brown rice with Perfectly Cooked Quinoa (page 52).

Rainbow Quinoa Salad

For the Dressing

3 tablespoons low-sodium soy sauce

1 tablespoon sesame oil

2 tablespoons lime juice

1 tablespoon Homemade Almond Butter (page 44)

2 tablespoons thinly sliced scallions

½ teaspoon grated ginger

2 garlic cloves, crushed

For the salad

3 cups Perfectly Cooked Quinoa (page 52)

1 cup chopped red cabbage

1 cup frozen edamame, defrosted

1 red bell pepper, chopped

½ cup chopped radish

½ cup chopped carrots

¼ cup chopped cilantro

⅓ cup chopped cashews

This nutrient-dense quinoa salad is packed with Asian flavors, lots of crunchy textures and plenty of beautiful colors. I love to add this salad to my weekend meal prep and then store it in airtight containers in the fridge for an easy grab-n-go lunch.

1   In a small bowl or spouted cup, combine the soy sauce, sesame oil, lime juice, almond butter, scallions, ginger, and garlic. Whisk together with a fork until everything is well combined. Set aside.

2   In a large bowl, combine the quinoa, cabbage, edamame, bell pepper, radish, and carrots.

3   Drizzle the dressing over the salad and gently toss everything together. Finish by stirring in the cilantro and cashews.

NUTRITION PER SERVING

314 calories

40g carbohydrates

11g protein

13g fat

6g fiber

Cauliflower Rice Pilaf

½ cup orzo pasta

1 teaspoon extra-virgin olive oil

2 tablespoons unsalted, pastured butter

½ cup diced onion

2 garlic cloves, chopped

3 cups frozen cauliflower rice, defrosted

1 cup low-sodium chicken broth

1 teaspoon sea salt

¼ teaspoon pepper

2 tablespoons Parmesan cheese

¼ cup chopped parsley

This cauliflower rice pilaf is the best of both worlds and an easy way to enjoy a veggie side dish that is substantial enough to take the place of rice. The secret is to add some orzo pasta into the cauliflower rice to give it the texture and flavor of a traditional rice pilaf.

1 Cook the orzo according to the package instructions. Drizzle with olive oil so it doesn't stick while you prepare the rest of the dish.

2 Melt the butter over medium heat in a large cast-iron or nonstick skillet. Add in the onion along with a pinch of salt and cook for 3 minutes, or until the onions are translucent.

3 Add the garlic and cook for 30 seconds before adding in the cauliflower rice, chicken broth, salt, and pepper. Simmer for 5 minutes, stir in the orzo and simmer for another 5 minutes, or until all the flavors have come together and everything is warmed through.

4 Finish with Parmesan cheese and fresh parsley. Serve and enjoy!

NUTRITION PER SERVING

105 calories

10.4g carbohydrates

3.5g protein

5.3g fat

2g fiber

LEVEL UP

This is a great side dish to serve with any weeknight meal! My family particularly loves this cauliflower rice pilaf served alongside my One Pan Creamy Chicken and Artichokes (page 226).

While this recipe is already veggie-packed, I can never resist an extra serving of dark leafy greens. Thinly slice one half cup of baby spinach and stir it in right in the end for an extra boost of nutrients and some beautiful color.

Easy Veggie Fried Quinoa

2 teaspoons toasted
 sesame oil

½ medium onion,
 chopped

2 garlic cloves, chopped

1 teaspoon grated ginger

1 red bell pepper,
 chopped

2 cups frozen mixed
 vegetables (I use peas,
 green beans, corn
 and carrots)

4 cups cooked Perfectly
 Cooked Quinoa
 (page 52)

5 scallions, plus extra for
 topping, finely chopped

4 tablespoons low-sodium
 soy sauce

2 eggs

½ cup egg whites

Sesame seeds, for
 topping (optional)

Veggie Fried Quinoa is a healthy spin on a Chinese takeout favorite, and it only takes 20 minutes to make. I love cooking the eggs in a separate pan and stirring them in right at the end to ensure they are light and fluffy.

1 Heat the sesame oil in a large nonstick skillet or cast-iron skillet over medium heat. Add in the onions, garlic, ginger, a pinch of salt and cook for 4–5 minutes, or until the onions are tender and translucent.

2 Stir in the red pepper and frozen vegetables and cook for another 5 minutes.

3 Add in the cooked quinoa, scallions, and soy sauce and stir until everything is well combined. Cook for an additional 5 minutes, or until everything is heated through.

4 In the meantime, whisk together eggs and egg whites. Coat a small nonstick pan with nonaerosol cooking spray and scramble your eggs until done.

5 Season with salt and pepper before adding the scrambled eggs into the fried quinoa skillet. Stir to combine and top with extra scallions and sesame seeds (if using).

**NUTRITION
PER SERVING**
375 calories
58g carbohydrates
20g protein
8g fat
10g fiber

LEVEL UP
Add an extra boost of protein to this meal by serving with my Crispy Baked Tofu (page 57) or adding some shredded Baked Bone-in Chicken Breast (page 54).

10 Seafood

Easy Fish Tacos

**For the Jalapeño
  and Cilantro Sauce**
1 garlic clove
½ cup 2% Greek yogurt
½ cup cilantro
¼ cup pickled jalapeños
2 teaspoons lime juice
¼ teaspoon kosher salt

For the Slaw
3 cups shredded cabbage
½ red onion, thinly sliced
⅓ cup chopped cilantro
½ lime juice
1 tablespoon extra-virgin
  olive oil
Pinch kosher salt

For the Fish
1 lb mahi mahi
½ teaspoon sea salt
¼ teaspoon black pepper
1 teaspoon olive oil
½ lime
8 corn tortillas
Serve with sliced radishes
  and extra cilantro, for
  even more flavor and
  texture.

These simple fish tacos are made with mahi mahi and served with a bright, fresh jalapeño and cilantro sauce and a crunchy citrus slaw. Each bite is like a little party in your mouth—cool, crunchy, creamy and super nutritious.

If you can't find mahi mahi, cod or tilapia would work well in this recipe. As always, use what you have and use what you love so you can make the recipes work for you and your lifestyle!

1 Combine the garlic, yogurt, pickled jalapeños, lime juice, and salt in a high-speed blender or food processor and blend until you have a bright, creamy sauce.

2 In a large bowl, combine the cabbage, onion, cilantro, lime juice, olive oil, and salt. Gently toss everything together and set aside.

3 Using a sharp knife, carefully remove the skin from the fish.

4 Cut mahi mahi in half horizontally and then slice into ½-inch (1cm) pieces.

5 Season both sides of the fish with salt, pepper, and smoked paprika.

6 Heat a large nonstick skillet and add olive oil to lightly coat the pan. Place fish in the pan and cook for 2–3 minutes on the first side, or until the fish is beginning to turn opaque from the bottom up.

7 Flip and cook for another 2–3 minutes or until cooked through. Give the fish a big squeeze of fresh lime and transfer to a plate.

8 Heat tortillas, one at a time, over an open flame on your stovetop to give them a charred flavor.

9 Layer slaw on the bottom of the tortilla. Top with a few pieces of fish and a drizzle of taco sauce. Serve and enjoy!

STORAGE When stored separately in airtight containers, all of the components will happily last in your fridge for up to 3 days.

**NUTRITION
PER SERVING**
284 calories
31g carbohydrates
28g protein
6g fat
5g fiber

LEVEL UP ───────────────────────────────
You can prep the sauce and slaw ahead of time to make meal time even easier. Save some extra time by using a bag of pre-cut coleslaw mix.

Thai Cod Coconut Curry

1 tablespoon coconut oil

½ medium onion,
    thinly sliced

1 tablespoon grated
    ginger

2 garlic cloves, chopped

1x 15-ounce (425g) can
    full-fat coconut milk

3 tablespoons red
    Thai curry paste

⅓ cup low-sodium
    vegetable broth

1 tablespoon fish sauce

1 tablespoon honey

1 cup cauliflower, cut into
    small florets

1 cup green beans, cut
    into 1-inch
    (2.5cm) pieces

1 red bell pepper, cut into
    strips and halved

2-3 carrots thinly sliced on
    a bias

1 ¼ lb cod, cut into 1-inch
    (2.5cm) pieces

Sea salt and pepper,
    to taste

2 tablespoons chopped
    cilantro

1-2 tablespoons fresh
    lime juice

This simple and flavorful meal tastes like it requires a lot more effort than it actually does. Feel free to swap in whatever vegetables you have on hand—broccoli, kale, butternut squash, and mushrooms would all be delicious. Just be sure to keep the veggies relatively small and about the same size so they cook evenly.

1 Heat the oil in a large cast-iron pan or a skillet with high sides. Add the onion, ginger and garlic, and cook until tender and fragrant, about 5 minutes.

2 Add in the coconut milk, curry paste, vegetable broth, fish sauce, and honey, and whisk until well combined. Add the veggies and bring everything to a boil. Reduce the heat to a simmer, cover and cook for 6–8 minutes or until veggies are tender but still al dente.

3 Lightly season the cod with salt and pepper, nestle the pieces into the pan, and spoon some of the sauce over top. Cover the pot and cook for 5 minutes, or until the fish is cooked through—the fish will be flaky and white all the way through.

4 Add fresh lime juice over top and sprinkle with cilantro. Serve on its own or with your favorite rice or whole grain.

**NUTRITION
PER SERVING**
433 calories
20g carbohydrates
30g protein
28g fat
4g fiber

LEVEL UP
Red curry paste is a sweet and savory combination of garlic, lemon grass, red chili, and other aromatic flavors. It's a simple way to add a lot of depth to this quick-cooking meal. It is available in most grocery stores, or you can find it online. If preferred, you can sub in green or yellow curry paste as well.

Roasted Shrimp and Green Beans

1 lb medium-large raw
shrimp (thawed if
frozen), peeled

1 lb green beans,
ends trimmed

2 tablespoons extra-virgin
olive oil, plus extra to
brush the pan

½ teaspoon coriander

½ teaspoon cumin

½ teaspoon sea salt

¾ teaspoon pepper

⅛ teaspoon cayenne
pepper

Zest from one lemon, save
the lemon and cut into
quarters

Roasted shrimp and green beans is an easy, healthy one-pan meal that
is packed with protein and veggies while being low-carb. The perfect
quick dinner idea for a busy weeknight, it's delicious, nutritious and
super family-friendly.

1 Preheat the oven to 425°F (220°C).

2 Once the shrimp has been peeled and cleaned, rinse it under cold
water. Be sure to pat the shrimp dry (if the shrimp is not dry it will
steam rather than roast).

3 Place the trimmed and cut beans in a bowl and toss with 1
tablespoon of the olive oil, the coriander, cumin, salt, pepper, and
cayenne pepper.

4 Place shrimp in another bowl with the remaining olive oil, lemon
zest, salt, and fresh ground black pepper.

5 Brush the roasting pan with olive oil or use a nonstick spray, then
arrange the beans on the pan in a single layer (as much as possible).
Roast beans for 10 minutes. After 10 minutes, toss the beans and
arrange shrimp on top and roast 8–10 minutes more or until shrimp
are just done.

6 Squeeze the lemon over the shrimp and beans and serve
immediately.

**NUTRITION
PER SERVING**
180 calories
9g carbohydrates
18g protein
9g fat
3g fiber

LEVEL UP ————————————————————

I like to leave the tails on the shrimp for this recipe as it adds more flavor to
the dish, but if preferred, you can remove them.

Short on time? Look for green beans that have been pre-washed and trimmed
at your grocery store.

20-Minute Garlicky Shrimp and Spinach

3 tablespoons extra-virgin olive oil

8–10 garlic cloves, finely chopped

1 lb baby spinach

1 lb shrimp, peeled and deveined, tails removed

Large pinch crushed red pepper flakes

Zest and juice of 1 lemon

Handful chopped parsley

Sea salt and pepper, to taste

If you love garlic, you'll adore this easy garlic and lemon shrimp dish served over a bed of freshly wilted spinach. This is a quick and simple recipe that is packed with flavor and can be enjoyed as is for a delicious low-carb meal, or you can create a heartier meal by serving with your favorite whole grain.

1 Heat 1 tablespoon of the olive oil in a large nonstick or enamel-coated pot. Add in half of the garlic along with a pinch of salt. Once the garlic is fragrant, add the spinach (it will seem like a lot of spinach, which is why I recommend using a pot, but as it cooks it will wilt down quite a bit) and toss until all the spinach is shiny and beginning to wilt down. Shut off the heat and place the pan on the back burner (the residual heat in the pan will finish cooking the spinach while you make the shrimp).

2 Heat the rest of the olive oil in a large nonstick skillet or cast-iron pan and add in the rest of the garlic along with a pinch of salt and the red pepper flakes. Once the garlic is fragrant, toss in the shrimp.

3 Stir periodically as the shrimp begins to turn opaque. They cook quickly and will be done in 3-4 minutes. Once they all turn opaque, turn off the heat and finish them with lemon zest, lemon juice, and parsley.

4 Arrange the spinach in a large, shallow bowl and top with the shrimp and all the garlicky sauce.

NUTRITION PER SERVING
224 calories
6g carbohydrates
26g protein
12g fat
1g fiber

LEVEL UP ——————

If using frozen shrimp, you'll want to defrost them before cooking. If you plan ahead, you can simply place the frozen package in a bowl in the fridge and they'll gradually thaw overnight. If you need them for the same day, place the unopened bag in a large bowl of cold water and top with a large plate to help keep the bag fully submerged. It should take about 30 minutes for your shrimp to defrost and be ready to cook.

Baked Flounder Parmesan

2 tablespoons extra-virgin olive oil

4 flounder fillets (1-1.5 lbs)

¼ teaspoon sea salt

¼ teaspoon black pepper

⅓ cup Parmesan cheese

⅓ cup panko bread crumbs

½ teaspoon garlic powder

1 tablespoon fresh thyme, chopped (or 1 teaspoon dried thyme)

Zest from one lemon

Non-aerosol cooking spray

Flounder is a delicious, thin, flaky white fish that cooks quickly and is perfect for busy weeknights. Each fillet is topped with nutty Parmesan cheese and crunchy panko bread crumbs seasoned with garlic, lemon and thyme. Serve this with my easy Weeknight Dinner Salad (page 104) and Dad's Broccoli Rabe (page 153).

1 Preheat your oven to 425°F (220°C) and coat a rimmed baking sheet with 1 tablespoon of the olive oil.

2 Pat the flounder fillets dry and place them on a prepared baking sheet. Lightly season each fillet with salt and pepper.

3 In a small bowl, combine the Parmesan cheese, panko, garlic powder, and fresh thyme. Drizzle in the remaining olive oil and mix with your fingers so the bread crumbs are slightly moistened.

4 Evenly divide the Parmesan mixture over the top of each flounder fillet. Spritz the top of each with cooking spray (this will help the breading to brown when cooking).

5 Bake for 10–20 minutes, depending on the thickness of your fish. When the fish is cooked through it will turn from translucent to opaque and flake easily with a fork. Serve with fresh lemon and enjoy!

NUTRITION PER SERVING
272 calories
4.8g carbohydrates
34g protein
11.3g fat
0.2g fiber

LEVEL UP

Sole, tilapia, and cod would all work well for this recipe. If using frozen fish, be sure to defrost it before cooking.

Lemon Sole with Spring Vegetables

2 tablespoons unsalted pastured butter, divided

1 tablespoon extra-virgin olive oil, plus extra for drizzling

1¼ lb sole, cut into 4 pieces

½ teaspoon sea salt, plus additional to taste

¼ teaspoon ground black pepper, plus additional to taste

1 medium yellow onion, chopped

2-3 carrots, cut into ½-inch pieces on a bias

1½ cups sugar snap peas, trimmed, halved on a bias

1 red bell pepper, cut into 1-inch (2.5cm) cubes

1 yellow squash, cut into quarter moons

2 cloves garlic, finely chopped

2 tablespoons fresh lemon juice

1 tablespoon chopped fresh flat-leaf parsley, plus additional for garnish

This was a recipe I found in Clean Eating magazine a few years back. I slightly adapted it to my personal taste, and it quickly became a keeper in our home. Remember, all recipes are a blueprint—a simple guide for you to follow as you adapt them to your personal preferences.

If you've never had it, sole is a light, sweet white fish that is easy to work with and it cooks very quickly. Pairing it with spring veggies makes for a stunning and delicious meal that is easy enough for a Tuesday night!

1 Preheat the oven to 200°F (95°C) and line a large baking sheet with parchment.

2 In a large skillet on medium-high, melt 1 tablespoon of butter with the oil. Add the onion, along with a pinch of salt, and cook, stirring occasionally, until just tender and translucent.

3 Add the carrots, snap peas, pepper, squash and garlic along with another pinch of salt and black pepper. Sauté until the veggies are tender, yet still crisp; this will take about 6 minutes. Finish with 1 tablespoon lemon juice and transfer to a rimmed baking sheet—place in the oven to stay warm while you make the fish.

4 Pat both sides of the fish dry. Season one side of the fish with salt and pepper. Melt the remaining butter in a skillet and lay the fish seasoned-side down. Season the opposite side of the fish and cook until golden, basting with butter mixture occasionally, 2 to 3 minutes. Flip and cook for another 2 to 3 minutes, finish with remaining lemon juice.

5 Remove veggies from the oven and serve fish fillets over the veggies. Top with fresh parsley and an extra drizzle of olive oil. Enjoy!

NUTRITION PER SERVING
304 calories
17.8g carbohydrates
34.4g protein
11.6g fat
4.8g fiber

LEVEL UP

If you cannot find sole, flounder would work just as well.

If spring veggies are not in season, serve this sole with my Dad's Broccoli Rabe (page 153) or Collard Greens with Onions and Raisins (page 150).

Cast-Iron Salmon with Crispy Skin

16 ounces (453g) salmon, cut into 4-ounce (113g) fillets

1 teaspoon ghee, coconut or avocado oil

1 teaspoon sea salt,

½ teaspoon pepper

Extra-virgin olive oil and lemon wedges, for serving (optional)

This crispy cast-iron salmon is an easy and delicious weeknight meal that we almost always have in our weekly dinner rotation. The collagen-rich salmon skin is sprinkled with sea salt and seared in a super-hot cast-iron skillet, creating a crispy, potato-chip-like texture. Enjoy this with your favorite veggie side and some Perfectly Cooked Brown Rice (page 51) or Perfectly Cooked Quinoa (page 52) for a simple and nourishing meal your entire family will enjoy.

1 Preheat the oven to 450°F (230°C) and place a 12-inch (30.5cm) cast-iron skillet in the oven to heat (this is going to help our salmon skin get nice and crispy).

2 Remove the salmon from the fridge at least 15 minutes before cooking so it can come to room temperature. Place the fish on a cutting board and use a paper towel to pat both sides of the salmon dry, absorbing any excess moisture. If the skin is wet, it won't get crispy when the salmon cooks.

3 Right before you are ready to cook the salmon, season the salmon skin generously with sea salt—this is going to create a crispy, salty skin on your salmon.

4 Carefully, remove the hot pan from the oven and melt the ghee in the pan. Arrange salmon in the pan, skin-side down—you want to hear a sizzling sear when it hits the pan.

5 Season the top of salmon with a little more salt and pepper, and place in the oven for about 15 minutes.

6 Once the salmon is opaque and flaky, it's ready to serve. I usually just stick a fork in and twist to make sure my salmon is done. The general rule is to cook for 4–6 minutes per every ½-inch (1cm) of thickness. So be sure to adjust cook time as needed. Top with a drizzle of extra-virgin olive oil and serve with lemon wedges.

NUTRITION PER SERVING
173 calories
1g carbohydrates
23g protein
8g fat
1g fiber

LEVEL UP
When shopping for salmon, look for Pacific salmon as this is primarily wild-caught salmon that are caught from oceans and rivers. Because wild salmon live in their natural habitat, they get a lot of exercise and eat a natural diet of krill, crabs, and shrimp, which provide much of the heart-healthy omega-3 fatty acids found in salmon. Examples of wild salmon include King, Coho, and Sockeye.

Salmon Burgers with Creamy Dill Yogurt Sauce

For the Dill Yogurt Sauce

½ cup plain nonfat Greek yogurt

1 garlic clove, crushed

2 tablespoons chopped dill

2 tablespoons fresh lemon juice

Pinch of sea salt and pepper

For the Salmon Burgers

1x 14.75-ounce (418g) can wild salmon*

¼ cup red onion, diced

¼ cup red pepper, diced

¼ cup chopped dill, packed

Zest and juice of 1 lemon

1 egg

⅓ cup oat flour

¼ teaspoon cayenne pepper

½ teaspoon sea salt

¼ teaspoon pepper

1 tablespoon coconut oil

4 sprouted English muffins or whole-grain buns

A few handfuls arugula

Flavorful, healthy, and protein-packed, these delicious salmon burgers come together in just 30 minutes making for a quick and easy lunch or dinner.

1 Combine the yogurt, garlic, dill, lemon juice, salt, and paper in a small bowl. Stir until well combined and set aside.

2 Combine the salmon, onion, red pepper, dill, lemon zest, lemon juice, egg, oat flour, cayenne pepper, salt, and pepper in a large bowl. Mix until well combined.

3 Use your hands to shape 4 burger patties (your burgers should be about 4 ounces (113g) each).

4 Heat coconut oil in a large nonstick pan over medium heat and cook the burgers for 4–5 minutes on each side, or until browned and crisp on the edges and heated through.

5 While your burgers are cooking, toast up your English muffins and then layer the bottom half of each with a handful of arugula.

6 Place the cooked salmon burger over the top of the arugula and top with 2 tablespoons of the creamy dill sauce before placing on the top of the muffin. Enjoy!

NUTRITION PER SERVING

354 calories

34g carbohydrates

37g protein

9g fat

5g fiber

LEVEL UP

*Canned salmon often comes with skin and little bones in the mix, don't be scared as they are all perfectly fine to eat (as a matter of fact, the little salmon bones are packed with calcium). Once you begin to mix everything together, the bones and skin break down and you don't even know they are there. Alternatively, you can look for skinless, boneless canned salmon.

Make this a veggie-packed, low-carb meal by skipping the bun and serving your salmon burger over my Creamy Crunchy Coleslaw (page 145).

11 Chicken & Turkey

Turkey Stuffed Peppers

6 bell peppers

2 teaspoons extra-virgin olive oil

1 medium yellow onion, chopped

4 garlic cloves, chopped

1 lb ground turkey

½ teaspoon sea salt

½ teaspoon pepper

1 teaspoon Italian seasoning

2 cups Perfectly Cooked Brown Rice (page 51)

1 cup frozen peas

1x 28-ounce (793g) can crushed tomatoes

6 tablespoons cheddar cheese, shredded

Growing up, stuffed peppers were a family staple in our house and one of my favorite dinners. It's an easy meal that is packed with protein, veggies and whole grains. They seem to get better as they sit, so they make great leftovers and are perfect for meal prep. My son loves this recipe so much that he often asks me to make this for his birthday dinner!

1 Preheat the oven to 350°F (180°C). Slice the bell peppers in half from top to bottom down through the stem. Remove the seeds and membranes.

2 Fill a large pot with water and bring to a boil. Drop the peppers in the boiling water and cook for 5 minutes (the water will not come back up to a boil). Remove the peppers from the water and lay on a clean dish towel to cool.

3 In a large nonstick skillet, heat the oil and add in the onion and garlic and season with salt, and pepper. Sauté for 4 minutes, or until the onions and garlic begin to look translucent. Push veggies aside, add ground turkey to the pan and season with a little more salt and pepper, and the Italian seasoning.

4 Slowly combine the meat and the veggies and cook until the turkey has browned. Stir in the brown rice and 1¼ cups of the crushed tomatoes. Stir and simmer for 5–10 minutes. Adjust seasonings as needed.

5 Spread 1 cup of the crushed tomatoes on the bottom of a 9x11-inch (22cm x 28cm) baking dish and arrange the peppers cut-side up in the dish. Scoop ½ cup of filling in each pepper (or enough to fill it up).

6 Top each pepper with a tablespoon of the remaining tomatoes and a sprinkle of shredded cheese.

7 Bake the peppers for 30 minutes, or until the cheese has melted and the peppers are heated through.

NUTRITION PER SERVING
319 calories
35g carbohydrate
27g protein
9g fat
7g fiber

LEVEL UP

Try swapping in ground beef, bison or chicken for the turkey. Look for organic and grass-fed options.

Swap out half of the brown rice with cauliflower rice. I do this all the time.

Greek-Style Turkey Burgers

For the Tzatziki Sauce

½ large English cucumber

1 cup plain 2%
Greek yogurt

1 garlic clove, crushed

1 tablespoon finely
chopped dill

1 tablespoon lemon juice

¼ teaspoon sea salt

¼ teaspoon lemon zest

1 teaspoon extra-virgin
olive oil

For the Burgers

1 lb ground turkey

1 tablespoon garlic
powder

1 tablespoon dried
oregano

½ teaspoon sea salt

¼ teaspoon pepper

¼ cup plain 2%
Greek yogurt

½ cup jarred roasted
peppers, chopped

¼ cup pitted Kalamata
olives, chopped

⅓ cup feta cheese,
crumbled

8 butter lettuce leaves

Easy, healthy and packed with flavor, these turkey burgers are great for cookouts and meal prep. I developed this recipe years ago when I was living in California and they still remain a staple in my home. Served in butter lettuce cups and topped with a creamy tzatziki sauce, these burgers are light, fresh, and so very delicious.

1 Prepare the sauce by grating the cucumber on the large holes of a box grater. Place the cucumber on a clean kitchen towel and gently squeeze out the excess water.

2 In a medium bowl, combine the cucumber, yogurt, garlic, dill, lemon juice and salt. Finish with lemon zest and a drizzle of olive oil.

3 Place turkey in a large bowl and add the garlic powder, oregano, salt, pepper, and yogurt.

4 Using your hands, combine until everything is well incorporated. Add peppers, olives and feta cheese to the turkey mixture and gently work into the meat until the ingredients are evenly distributed. Form 4 equal-sized burger patties.

5 Heat grill or grill pan over a medium heat and place burgers on the pan. Grill for 4–6 minutes per side or until cooked through.

6 Place burgers on top of two layered leaves of butter lettuce and finish with a couple tablespoons of sauce.

STORAGE Store any leftover turkey burgers in an airtight container in the refrigerator for up to 4 days. Reheat them in the microwave, on the grill pan or in a skillet.

Place any leftover tzatziki in an airtight container for freshness and it will keep in the fridge for 4–5 days. After the dip has been in the refrigerator for a bit, it may accumulate liquid on top. Simply stir it right back in before serving.

**NUTRITION
PER SERVING**

241 calories

10g carbohydrates

35g protein

7g fat

1.2g fiber

Baked Turkey Spinach Meatballs

2 lbs ground turkey (I use a combination of extra lean and regular)

½ small onion, finely chopped

8 ounces (226g) cremini mushrooms, finely chopped

10 ounces (283g) frozen spinach, defrosted and strained of excess water

½ cup Parmesan cheese

½ cup panko bread crumbs, gluten-free if desired

1 egg, beaten

2 egg whites (¼ cup)

1 teaspoon grated nutmeg

1½ teaspoons kosher salt

1 teaspoon pepper

4 cups jarred tomato sauce

Light, tender and packed with flavor, this easy baked meatball recipe is loaded with protein and vegetables. The secret to moist turkey meatballs is minced mushrooms. I love to serve these meatballs over a bed of Roasted Spaghetti Squash (page 154) for a veggie-packed, high-protein dinner, and they also work great for meal prep.

1 Preheat the oven to 400°F (200°C) and line 2 rimmed baking sheets with parchment paper (or spray with cooking spray).

2 Add ground turkey to a large bowl along with the onion, mushrooms, spinach, Parmesan cheese, breadcrumbs, egg, egg whites, nutmeg, salt, and pepper. Use your hands to gently combine all the ingredients together.

3 Scoop a heaping tablespoon of the mixture into your palm and roll into a ball. If the mixture is very sticky, wet your hands to make this process easier.

4 Place the meatball on the prepared baking sheet and repeat until you have used all the meat. You should have about 40 meatballs when done.

5 Bake for 20 minutes or until the internal temperature of the meatballs reaches 165°F (175°C).

6 When ready to serve, heat the tomato sauce in a large sauté pan or shallow pot (I like to use my cast-iron skillet) and transfer cooked meatballs into the sauce. Simmer for 5–10 minutes, top with extra Parmesan, serve and enjoy!

STORAGE These meatballs will last in an airtight container in your refrigerator for up to 5 days, and up to 3 months when stored in the freezer.

NUTRITION PER SERVING
231 calories
14g carbohydrates
35g protein
5g fat
4g fiber

LEVEL UP ────────────────────

Ground turkey can easily be swapped with ground chicken, bison, or grass-fed beef. As always, use what you have and love.

The mushrooms are the secret to keeping these lean meatballs super moist and tender. They won't make the meatballs taste like mushrooms; I promise!

I often bake the meatballs on the weekend and then warm them in the sauce during the week.

Turkey and Zucchini Skillet

1 lb ground turkey

1 tablespoon extra-virgin olive oil

4–5 garlic cloves, chopped

1 medium onion, chopped

4 small-medium zucchinis. chopped

2x 15-ounce (425g) cans diced tomatoes

1 tablespoon Italian seasoning

Sea salt and pepper, to taste

Parmesan cheese, for serving (optional)

Crushed red pepper flakes, for serving (optional)

This easy and nutritious dish is loaded with protein and vegetables, simple to make and perfect for a family meal on a busy weeknight. It's also a great option for meal prep as it will last in your fridge for up to 5 days. You can serve this on its own, over Perfectly Cooked Brown Rice (page 51) or Perfectly Cooked Quinoa (page 52), cauliflower rice, or my personal favorite: a bed of Roasted Spaghetti Squash (page 154).

1   Heat a large nonstick skillet over medium heat and add oil. Once the olive oil is hot, stir in the onion and garlic along with a pinch of salt. Let them cook for 2 minutes, or until onions are fragrant and beginning to look translucent.

2   Push all the veggies to one side of the pan and then, using a wooden or rubber spatula, stir in ground turkey and break into small pieces. Season the turkey with salt and pepper.

3   Once the turkey has lost its pink color, combine the ground turkey with the onions and garlic.

4   Add in zucchini, Italian seasoning, a little more salt and pepper, and tomatoes. Give it a good mix and allow everything to simmer for 15–30 minutes, depending on how soft you like your zucchini.

5   Serve over a bed of spaghetti squash (or pasta, rice, or cauliflower rice) and top with some red pepper flakes and Parmesan cheese, if using.

NUTRITION PER SERVING
246 calories
19g carbohydrates
31g protein
7g fat
5g fiber

LEVEL UP
While this recipe calls for ground turkey, you can use any type of ground meat you prefer. Ground beef, bison, and chicken would all be great options.

If you want to keep this recipe super lean, opt for extra-lean ground turkey! I always recommend buying organic meats when you can as an easy way to level up the quality of your ingredients.

Baked Buffalo Chicken Meatballs

1 lb lean ground chicken

1 egg

½ cup panko
  bread crumbs

½ cup frozen cauliflower
  rice, defrosted

½ teaspoon onion powder

½ teaspoon garlic powder

½ teaspoon smoked
  paprika

½ teaspoon sea salt

½ teaspoon pepper

¼ cup chopped parsley

½ cup buffalo wing sauce

Carrot sticks, celery sticks
  and blue cheese
  dressing or crumbles,
  for serving (optional)

Buffalo-inspired recipes are very popular in our home and these meatballs are no exception. This is a fun and delicious recipe to serve at a party or for game day, and it's equally delightful for a quick, high-protein, weeknight dinner. Serve with your favorite veggie or whole grain to round out the meal.

1 Preheat the oven to 400°F (200°C). Line a rimmed baking sheet with a silpat mat or parchment paper and set aside.

2 In a large bowl, combine the ground chicken, egg, breadcrumbs, cauliflower rice, onion powder, garlic powder, smoked paprika, salt, pepper, and parsley. Use your hands to mix everything together until just incorporated.

3 Grab a hearty tablespoon of the mixture and roll in between the palms of your hand to form a ball. If the dough feels sticky, wet your palms with cool water as this will make it easier to roll the meatballs.

4 Place on a prepared baking sheet and repeat until you have rolled all the meatballs.

5 Bake in the oven for 20 minutes. In the meantime, warm the buffalo wing sauce in a medium nonstick skillet.

6 Remove the meatballs from the oven and transfer to the saucepan. Toss in the buffalo sauce until lightly coated. Serve with carrots, celery and blue cheese dressing.

**NUTRITION
PER SERVING**
217 calories
8g carbohydrates
23g protein
11g fat
1g fiber

One-Pan Creamy Chicken and Artichokes

1½ lb boneless, skinless chicken thighs, trimmed (6-8 depending on size)

½ teaspoon sea salt

½ teaspoon pepper

3 tablespoons arrowroot powder

1½ tablespoons extra-virgin olive oil, divided

1x 14-ounce (396g) can full-fat coconut milk

½ medium red onion, quartered and thinly sliced (1 cup)

2 garlic cloves, thinly sliced

1x 14-ounce (396g) can quartered artichoke hearts, drained

1 cup low-sodium chicken broth

Zest of 1 lemon

¼ teaspoon crushed red pepper flakes

4 sprigs of thyme

This dairy-free, creamy artichoke chicken skillet is quick and easy comfort food at its best. I found a version of this recipe in a clean eating magazine, and it quickly became a family staple in our house. We love to serve this over my Cauliflower Rice Pilaf (page 196) but it's also delicious with Perfectly Cooked Quinoa (page 52), Perfectly Cooked Brown Rice (page 51), or couscous.

1   Season the chicken with half of the salt and pepper. Place the arrowroot powder in a shallow bowl and the dredge chicken, shaking off the excess.

2   Heat a large nonstick skillet over medium heat and add 1 tablespoon of the oil. Add the chicken to the skillet and cook for 3–4 minutes per side, until browned. Transfer to a plate and set aside.

3   Add the coconut milk to a blender and blend to combine the solids and water until creamy.

4   Reduce heat to medium and add the remaining oil. Add the onion and cook for 2 minutes, or until soft. Add the garlic and cook for 30 seconds. Add the artichokes, broth, coconut milk, lemon zest, red pepper flakes, thyme, and remaining salt and pepper. Bring to a simmer.

5   Return chicken to the skillet and simmer everything on low for 12–15 minutes, until the chicken is cooked through and the sauce has slightly reduced. Remove thyme sprigs.

6   Divide chicken, vegetables and sauce among the plates. Serve and enjoy!

NUTRITION PER SERVING
279 calories
7g carbohydrates
33g protein
12g fat
1g fiber

LEVEL UP

Arrowroot powder is a flavorless thickener similar to cornstarch that helps to make the sauce thick and creamy. If you can't find arrowroot, simply swap in cornstarch.

Full-fat coconut milk is often solidified in the can. I like to add the coconut milk to my blender to create a smooth texture before adding it into the pan.

BBQ Chicken-Stuffed Sweet Potatoes

2 lbs boneless, skinless
  chicken breast
1½ cups barbecue sauce
Creamy Crunchy Coleslaw
  (page 145)
4 sweet potatoes
Sea salt and pepper,
  to taste

For BBQ sauce
1x 15-ounce (425g) can
  tomato sauce
¼ cup tomato paste
½ cup apple cider vinegar
¼ cup honey
¼ tablespoon molasses
3 tablespoons
  Worcestershire sauce
1 teaspoon chipotle
  powder
1 teaspoon garlic powder
½ teaspoon onion powder
1 pinch cayenne pepper,
  plus more to taste
½ teaspoon sea salt
½ teaspoon pepper

This shredded barbeque chicken is a staple in our home because it's easy peasy and everyone gobbles it up. I often make this chicken when I am doing my meal prep, so I have it on hand to layer into a taco or quesadilla, serve over a salad, or stuff into a sweet potato. I love pairing the smoky flavors of this chicken with my cool and Creamy Crunchy Coleslaw (page 145) but you can also top these chicken stuffed potatoes with some homemade Guacamole (page 90).

1 Place the chicken in a single layer on the bottom of your slow cooker. Pour the sauce over the chicken, making sure that all the chicken is coated. Set your heat to high and cook for 3½ hours.

2 Carefully remove the chicken and shred it apart using 2 forks. Place the chicken back in the slow cooker and cook for another 30 minutes.

3 In the meantime, prepare your coleslaw and store in the fridge in an airtight container until ready to eat.

4 About 1 hour before mealtime, preheat your oven to 400°F (200°C). Give your sweet potatoes a good wash under cold water.

5 Place the sweet potatoes on a rimmed baking sheet and poke 4–5 holes in each sweet potato with a fork or sharp knife.

6 Bake in the oven for 50–60 minutes, or until soft. To test if they're done, poke them with a fork or knife which will easily insert when the potatoes are ready.

7 Split each sweet potato in half and top each half with shredded BBQ chicken and a scoop of coleslaw.

BBQ SAUCE
Whisk all ingredients together in a medium saucepan. Bring to a low boil, then reduce heat to medium-low and simmer (uncovered) for 20 minutes, or until the sauce has slightly thickened.

NUTRITION PER SERVING
333 calories
49g carbohydrates
28g protein
8g fat
5g fiber

Easy Chicken and Broccoli Quesadillas

1 heaping cup broccoli
  florets

1 cup rotisserie chicken,
  skin and bones removed
  and chopped

½ teaspoon cumin

½ teaspoon garlic powder

Salt and pepper, to taste

2 8-inch sprouted tortillas
  (or whatever type of
  tortilla you prefer)

½ cup shredded cheddar
  cheese

½ cup plain 2% Greek
  yogurt (optional)

1-2 tablespoons sriracha
  (optional)

Quesadillas are an easy go-to weeknight staple in our home. While chicken and broccoli is one of my favorite quesadilla combinations, you can make this recipe using all different types of fillings. It's a perfect way to use up any leftovers you have hanging out in the fridge, so as always, use what you have and use what you love!

1 Add an inch of water to a large nonstick sauté pan and place the broccoli florets on top.

2 Turn the heat on high and bring the water to a boil. Cover the pot and let the water continue to boil for 3-4 minutes or until the broccoli is vibrant and tender. Carefully strain the water and finely chop the steamed broccoli once cool enough to handle.

3 Place your saucepan back on the burner over a medium-low heat. Add the chopped chicken and broccoli and season with cumin, garlic powder, salt and pepper. Stir together and cook for 3-4 minutes, or until everything is heated through. Transfer seasoned meat and veggies into a small bowl.

4 Place one tortilla in the hot, dry pan and gently heat for 20-30 seconds or until heated. Flip the tortilla and layer 2 tablespoons of cheese over one half of the tortilla followed by half the chicken and broccoli and another 2 tablespoons of cheese.

5 Using a spatula, fold the tortilla over onto itself to form a half moon and top with another pan or teapot to help hold it down (you can also push down with your spatula for a minute). Cook for 2 minutes or until the bottom is lightly browned. Flip the tortilla and cook for another 2 minutes or until both sides are lightly browned and cheese is melted. Remove from the pan, cool, and cut in half.

OPTIONAL DIPPING SAUCE ————————————————

Combine Greek yogurt and sriracha sauce to create a cool and spicy dip for your quesadilla.

**NUTRITION
PER SERVING**
363 calories
30g carbohydrates
32g protein
13g fat
3g fiber

LEVEL UP ————————————————

Quesadillas are also delicious topped with Guacamole (page 90) and/or Pico De Gallo (page 88). My family loves when I serve quesadillas with a variety of toppings—it turns dinner into a fun quesadilla party!

Oven-Baked Chicken Wings

3-3½ lbs chicken wings, split

3 tablespoons aluminum-free baking powder

¾ teaspoon sea salt, divided

½ teaspoon pepper

½ teaspoon garlic powder

½ teaspoon onion powder

½ teaspoon smoked paprika

My husband has an undying love for chicken wings that he has passed down to both of our children. It's a love that's easy to understand as wings are an easy, fun, and delicious food that you get to eat with your hands. The addition of baking powder helps to draw the moisture out the wings, which results in a crispier baked chicken wing without the need to deep fry. Sometimes we serve them with buffalo sauce or Barbecue Sauce (see page 228) on the side, but usually my family requests them as is—dry and well-seasoned, straight from the oven.

1 Place your oven rack in the center of the oven and preheat to 425°F (220°C).

2 Line a rimmed baking sheet with aluminum foil and place a wire rack on top. Spray the rack with cooking spray.

3 Pat the chicken wings dry, using paper towels. It's important for the wings to be very dry or they will steam in the oven and will not crisp up. Transfer wings to a large bowl.

4 Combine the baking powder, a ½ teaspoon of the salt, and the black pepper, garlic powder, onion powder, and smoked paprika in a small bowl. Sprinkle the seasoning over the wings until all the wings are lightly coated with the seasoning.

5 Place wings in a single layer, skin-side up on the prepared wire rack. Sprinkle them with the remaining salt.

6 Bake for 45-50 minutes, flipping halfway through, or until the wings are crisp and golden brown and the internal temperature has reached 165°F (75°C).

NUTRITION PER SERVING
274 calories
1g carbohydrates
22g protein
20g fat
0.4g fiber

LEVEL UP

Don't forget your veggies! Serve with an Easy Weeknight Dinner Salad (page 104) or with fresh vegetables from your Spies Family Crudité (page 47) and Greek Yogurt Veggie Dip (page 93).

12 Sweet Treats & Snacks

6-Ingredient Banana Oatmeal Energy Bars

3 large, ripe bananas
2 cups old-fashioned rolled oats
1 cup creamy, all-natural peanut butter
1 cup walnuts, chopped
½ cup chocolate chips
1 teaspoon vanilla extract
1 teaspoon cinnamon

The Clean & Delicious family loves bananas and oatmeal! Some of my most popular recipes include this dynamic duo, including my 3-ingredient Banana Oatmeal Cookies (page 71) and my Banana Oatmeal and Pancakes (page 76). Add peanut butter to the mix and suddenly things get even tastier. This recipe has a softer texture than a traditional crunchy energy bar, which I love.

1 Preheat the oven to 350°F (180°C) and grease a quarter sheet pan with cooking spray or coconut oil.

2 Place the bananas in a large bowl and mash with the back of a fork until they are broken down.

3 Add the oats, peanut butter, chopped walnuts, chocolate chips, vanilla, and cinnamon.

4 Stir everything together until all the ingredients are well combined, and you have a nice thick batter.

5 Transfer the batter onto the prepared sheet pan and pat down until it's pushed into the corners, along the sides and even on top.

6 Bake for 25–30 minutes or until they are fragrant, lightly browned on top and set through.

7 Cool completely. Slice into 16 bars by making 1 vertical slice and 7 horizontal ones.

STORAGE Stack the bars in an airtight container with parchment paper in between so they don't stick. They will last up to 1 week in the fridge and several months in the freezer.

NUTRITION PER SERVING
233 calories
21g carbohydrates
7g protein
15g fat
3g fiber

LEVEL UP

Be sure to use room-temperature peanut butter for this recipe as it will be much easier to work with.

Stir some flax seeds and pumpkin seeds into the mixture to give these energy bars an extra nutritional boost, or better yet, become a mad scientist and create your own flavor combinations!

No Bake Energy Bites

1 cup old-fashioned rolled oats

½ cup flaxseed meal (ground flax seeds)

½ cup all-natural crunchy peanut butter

⅓ cup honey

1 teaspoon vanilla extract

½ cup mini chocolate chips

These easy energy bites are made with 6 simple ingredients, naturally sweetened with honey, and filled with delicious mini chocolate chips. Think of them as a bite-sized granola bar that tastes just like raw cookie dough. They make for a lovely, nourishing snack or treat, are great for meal prep and are super kid friendly! I love to pack a small container of these little bites whenever my family and I go out for a weekend hike or plan to take a long car ride. Not only are they delicious, but they will keep you energized and fueled for hours.

1 Combine oats, ground flax eed, peanut butter, honey, and chocolate chips; mix well until all the ingredients are combined and you have a nice, hearty batter. It should stick together when pinched between your fingers.

2 Scoop up one teaspoon of dough, squash it together and roll between your palms to create a small ball. Place on a rimmed baking sheet and repeat until you have 16 energy bites.

3 Place in the fridge for 1 hour to set up and then transfer to an airtight container.

STORAGE These energy bites will last up to 5 days when stored in the fridge and up to 3 months when stored in the freezer.

LEVEL UP

Use this recipe as a blueprint and then make it your own! Sub in any type of seed or nut butter for the peanut butter and change up the mix-ins. Try raisins, shredded coconut, dried cranberries in place of the chocolate chips or better yet, create your own flavor combination.

Add a couple tablespoons of chia or hemp seeds to the batter to increase the nutrient density of these bars and add more fiber, protein, and healthy fat.

Look for certified organic rolled oats when shopping for oatmeal! This guarantees you will avoid any unwanted herbicides and is an easy way to level up the quality of your oatmeal.

NUTRITION PER SERVING
115 calories
13g carbohydrates
3g protein
6g fat
2g fiber

Beng Beng Banana Cake

For the Cake
3 large ripe bananas
¾ cup coconut sugar
2 eggs
2 tablespoons unsalted
  butter, softened
1 teaspoon vanilla extract
1 cup white whole
  wheat flour
1 teaspoon cinnamon
1 teaspoon baking soda
½ teaspoon kosher salt

For the Icing
6 ounces (170g)
  cream cheese
2 tablespoons plain
  2% Greek yogurt
2 tablespoons
  maple syrup
⅛ teaspoon banana
  extract (optional)

My husband, Beng, grew up eating the Sara Lee Banana Cake—he loved it so much that he would request it as his birthday cake each year. Needless to say, I wanted to make him a Clean & Delicious version of the classic cake he enjoyed so much growing up, so we could continue the tradition. To this day, this is the recipe he requests for his birthday each year—it's a moist, flavorful snack cake topped with a cream cheese icing. I always bake this cake in a square pan as that's how Sara Lee did it.

1 Preheat the oven to 325°F (170°C).

2 Grease an 8x8-inch (20cm x 20cm) baking pan with cooking spray, butter, or cooking oil.

3 Place bananas in a large bowl and mash with the back of a fork until they are broken down.

4 Add in coconut sugar, eggs, butter, and vanilla and mix by hand or with a hand mixer until combined.

5 Add in white whole wheat flour, cinnamon, baking soda and salt. Mix until everything is well incorporated and you have a nice, thick batter.

6 Pour the batter into the prepared baking pan and bake for 40–45 minutes or until fragrant and set through. Cool.

7 To make the icing, combine cream cheese, Greek yogurt, maple syrup and banana extract (if using) in a medium bowl. Beat with a hand mixer until light and fluffy.

8 Spread over cooled cake and chill for a minimum of 2 hours for the icing to set up (we always serve this cake chilled from the refrigerator).

LEVEL UP

This cake can also be made in a loaf pan. Just cook it for an extra 5-10 minutes or so, until the bread is set in the center.

The browner the bananas, the sweeter they will be. Be sure to use super-ripe bananas for this recipe.

Banana extract has a very strong flavor so you just need a little bit. The cream cheese icing is delicious with or without it.

White whole wheat flour has a mild flavor, which makes it perfect for baking.

NUTRITION PER SERVING
247 calories
35.2g carbohydrates
5.3g protein
10.1g fat
2.8g fiber

Double Chocolate Banana Bread

2 cups extra-fine almond flour

6 tablespoons cocoa powder

1½ teaspoons baking powder

½ teaspoon baking soda

½ teaspoon sea salt

3 large ripe bananas

2 eggs

¼ cup maple syrup

1 teaspoon vanilla extract

½ cup chocolate chips

I always buy extra bananas, so I have them browning on the counter, ready to make banana cookies, banana snack cake, and of course, this double chocolate banana bread! This recipe takes banana bread to a whole new level using a combination of cocoa powder and chocolate chips to deliver double chocolate-y goodness! It's made with almond flour, which is gluten free, and is naturally sweetened with maple syrup. This is a moist, tender, decadent banana bread that could easily be served for breakfast or dessert!

1 Preheat the oven to 350°F (180°C). Line a loaf pan with parchment paper.

2 In a large bowl, whisk together the almond flour, cocoa powder, baking powder, baking soda, and salt.

3 Place the bananas in a medium bowl. Use a potato masher or fork to mash the bananas until they're almost smooth.

4 Add the eggs, maple syrup, and vanilla to the bananas and mix until combined.

5 Pour the wet ingredients into the dry ingredients and stir until just combined. Add half of the chocolate chips and stir them in.

6 Carefully pour the batter into the prepared loaf pan. Sprinkle the remaining chocolate chips evenly over the top of the batter.

7 Bake for 45–50 minutes, or until the bread is fragrant and set through the center. Cool completely. Remove from the loaf pan, slice and enjoy.

STORAGE This chocolate banana bread can be kept covered with foil or plastic wrap at room temperature for 1 to 2 days, then I recommend transferring it to the fridge or freezer. I think it actually tastes best cold!

You can double the recipe to have a whole extra loaf to freeze, or freeze leftover slices of bread for up to 3 months. Tightly wrap either the whole loaf or individual slices in plastic wrap, then place in a resealable bag and freeze. Thaw your bread at room temperature when you're ready to eat.

NUTRITION PER SERVING

205 calories

22g carbohydrates

6g protein

12g fat

4g fiber

LEVEL UP —————————————————————————

Swap the eggs with 2 chia or flax seed eggs. Simply combine 2 tablespoons ground chia or flax seeds with six tablespoons of water. Let it sit for 5 minutes.

Chocolate Avocado Brownies

1 large, ripe avocado,
   pitted and flesh
   removed
½ cup mashed banana (or
   apple sauce)
½ cup maple syrup
1 teaspoon vanilla extract
3 large eggs
½ cup coconut flour
½ cup unsweetened cocoa
   powder
¼ teaspoon sea salt
1 teaspoon baking soda
⅓ cup chocolate chips

Rich and fudgy avocado brownies are an easy-to-make, gluten-free dessert, using avocado in place of oil or butter. They are lightly sweetened with ripe bananas and maple syrup, creating a nutrient-dense brownie that your whole family will love. I love having these brownies on hand to pack in lunch boxes for the school year because they provide a fun, sweet treat that won't leave my kids with a sugar crash!

1 Preheat the oven to 350°F (176°C) and grease an 8in x 8in (20cm x 20cm) baking dish.

2 In a food processor or blender, combine the avocado, banana, maple syrup, and vanilla.

3 Transfer to a large bowl and add in the eggs, coconut flour, cocoa powder, sea salt, and baking soda and mix with a hand blender until combined.

4 Pour mixture into the greased baking dish and sprinkle chocolate chips over the top.

5 Bake for about 25 minutes, or until set through.

6 Allow to cool completely before cutting. Cut into 9 squares and enjoy.

STORAGE Leftovers can be stored on the counter for up to 48 hours, or in the fridge in an airtight container for up to 1 week, or in the freezer for up to 3 months.

**NUTRITION
PER SERVING**
191 calories
28g carbohydrates
5g protein
8g fat
6g fiber

LEVEL UP ———————————————————————————————

This recipe is gently sweetened by the bananas, maple syrup, and chocolate chips sprinkled over the top. If you would like a little extra sweetness, stir a handful of extra chocolate chips into the batter as well.

Recipes can always be adapted to fit your dietary needs. For instance, if you want to keep this recipe 100% plant based, experiment with using flax or chia eggs and look for a dairy-free chocolate chip. If you need to cut back on sugar, look for a chocolate chip sweetened with monk fruit or stevia.

prep **10 minutes** / cook **12 minutes** / makes **20 servings**

Chocolate Chunk Cookies

1 cup all-natural almond butter

¾ cup coconut sugar

1 egg

1 teaspoon vanilla extract

1 teaspoon baking soda

1 teaspoon kosher salt

3 ounces (85g) dark chocolate, chopped

This has been my go-to chocolate chip cookie recipe for years. It is a gluten-free recipe that is grain and flour free—instead, it uses almond butter for the base. Whenever I make these chocolate chunk cookies, someone asks me for the recipe because they are just that good. You're going to want to keep this one in rotation!

1 Preheat the oven to 350°F (180°C).

2 Combine the almond butter, coconut sugar, egg, vanilla, baking soda, and salt in a large bowl and hand mix until everything is incorporated.

3 Gently stir in the chopped chocolate.

4 Drop cookie dough into tablespoon-sized scoops on a rimmed baking sheet lined with either a silpat or parchment paper.

5 Bake for 10–12 minutes or until lightly browned and set through. Cool completely and enjoy.

STORAGE Place the cookies in an airtight container and store them in the fridge for up to 5 days, or in the freezer for up to 3 months. You can also leave them on the counter for up to 3 days.

LEVEL UP

When buying natural nut butters—you may notice a pool of oil at the top of the jar when you open it, this is completely normal. Be sure to stir the nut butter well until the oil is mixed in and you have a nice, creamy, almost pourable consistency. If the nut butter is super dry or super oily, you may have a hard time forming your cookies.

I have made this recipe with other nut butters as well and it works out great. Feel free to use what you have and what you love.

Be sure to choose a good quality chocolate bar for this recipe. I love the 72% dark chocolate bar from Trader Joe's. I always keep a few in my pantry just for this recipe.

NUTRITION PER SERVING
126 calories
10g carbohydrates
3g protein
9g fat
2g fiber

prep **10 minutes** / cook **0 minutes** / makes **8 servings**

Frozen Banana Snickers Bars

2 medium-large bananas

¼ cup natural peanut butter

¼ cup chopped roasted peanuts

¼ cup chocolate chips

1½ teaspoons coconut oil

¼ teaspoon sea salt

This delightfully delicious, sweet treat tastes a lot like a Snickers bar but actually it's a frozen banana dipped in melted chocolate and coated in roasted peanuts. I love keeping these in the freezer to have on hand when a sweet craving strikes.

1 Line a quarter sheet pan with parchment paper and set aside.

2 Peel and slice each banana in half lengthwise, and then horizontally, so you have four quarters.

3 Evenly spread peanut butter amongst all 8 banana pieces and sprinkle half of the chopped peanuts over top.

4 Add chocolate chips to a small microwave-safe bowl and microwave on low in 20-second intervals until melted. Add in coconut oil and stir well.

5 Drizzle half the melted chocolate over the peanut butter, top with remaining peanuts and then drizzle the remaining chocolate over the top. Sprinkle with sea salt.

6 Place in the freezer for 2 hours or until set, and enjoy.

STORAGE Transfer remaining bars into an airtight container and store in the freezer for up to 1 month.

NUTRITION PER SERVING

139 calories

14g carbohydrates

4g protein

9g fat

2g fiber

LEVEL UP

This snack works with any type of nut or seed butter, so use what you have and love! Cashew butter, almond butter and sunflower seed butter would all be great options.

Add a superfood boost to these frozen bars by sprinkling some goji berries, cacao nibs, hemp seeds, or chia seeds over the top before popping them in the freezer.

Clean & Delicious **245**

Gluten-Free Carrot Cake

For the Cake
1 cup blanched almond
  flour
¼ cup coconut flour
2 tablespoons tapioca
  flour
1 teaspoon baking soda
½ teaspoon kosher salt
1 teaspoon cinnamon
⅛ teaspoon allspice
1 cup grated carrots (2-3
  carrots depending on
  their size)
3 eggs
⅓ cup coconut oil, melted
⅓ cup maple syrup
1 teaspoon vanilla extract

For the Frosting
¾ cup plain 2%
  Greek yogurt
¼ cup whipped cream
  cheese
1 tablespoon maple syrup

Fluffy, flavorful and perfectly spiced, you would never know this was a nutrient-dense, gluten-free carrot cake! While I like to keep things super simple in the kitchen (especially when it comes to baking), I have discovered that the combination of almond flour, coconut flour, and tapioca flour creates a moist and delicious base for gluten-free breads and cakes. I finish it off with a rich and creamy frosting made of Greek yogurt, cream cheese, and maple syrup.

1 Preheat the oven to 350°F (180°C).

2 Grease an 8in x 8in (20cm x 20cm) baking dish with coconut oil, butter, or cooking spray.

3 In a large bowl, combine almond flour, coconut flour, tapioca flour, baking soda, salt, cinnamon, and allspice. Gently toss everything together.

4 In a separate bowl, combine grated carrots, eggs, coconut oil, maple syrup, and vanilla extract. Whisk until well combined.

5 Add the wet ingredients to the dry and mix until all the ingredients are just incorporated.

6 Transfer batter to a greased pan and pop in the oven for 30 minutes or until cooked through. Cool completely.

7 Combine yogurt, cream cheese and maple syrup in a medium-sized bowl and mix well with a hand mixer. Be sure to get out all the lumps and bumps, mixing until you have a smooth, creamy icing. Spoon over the top of the cooled carrot cake and spread into an even layer.

**NUTRITION
PER SERVING**
229 calories
19g carbohydrates
6g protein
15g fat
2g fiber

LEVEL UP ─────────────────
Tapioca flour is a natural thickener that helps to keep the texture of this cake nice and light and fluffy. It's easy to find at grocery stores or online, but when in a pinch, you can substitute arrowroot or cornstarch.

Add an extra layer of flavor by stirring one teaspoon of orange zest right into your frosting. Beautiful and so delicious!

Best Blueberry Crisp

5 cups blueberries (about 2 lbs)

½ teaspoon lemon zest

2 tablespoons fresh lemon juice

2 tablespoons tapioca flour

¾ cup gluten-free rolled oats

¾ cup almond flour

½ cup roasted almonds, chopped

⅓ cup maple syrup

¼ cup coconut oil

1 teaspoon cinnamon

½ teaspoon sea salt

Fruit crisps are one of my favorite types of dessert, and this delightfully delicious gluten-free blueberry crisp is no exception. Finished with a sweet oat-almond crisp topping and filled with sweet, plump juicy blueberries, this is a recipe you will find yourself making again and again. It's super easy and I love that it can be prepared in advance, then baked right before serving.

1 Preheat the oven to 350°F (180°C).

2 Place blueberries in a 9in x 9in (23cm x 23 cm) baking dish. Add in the lemon zest, lemon juice, and tapioca flour. Gently toss together.

3 In a separate bowl, combine the rolled oats, almond flour, chopped almonds, maple syrup, coconut oil, cinnamon, and salt. Mix until everything is well incorporated.

4 Distribute the crisp topping over the blueberries, covering the surface of the pan.

5 Bake for 50 minutes or until the top is golden brown and the blueberries are hot and bubbly.

6 Serve hot, cold or room temperature as is or topped with Greek yogurt or vanilla ice cream.

STORAGE You can prepare this crisp ahead of time and store it in the fridge for up to 24 hours. Once ready to bake, bring to room temperature before baking.

NUTRITION PER SERVING
251 calories
28g carbohydrates
5g protein
15g fat
4g fiber

LEVEL UP ———————————————

Tapioca flour is a natural thickener. If you don't have any on hand, you can sub in cornstarch or arrowroot powder.

I love giving this crisp an extra flavor boost by adding 1 tablespoon of fresh ginger in with the blueberries. Ginger has a warm, spicy flavor and powerful anti-inflammatory and antioxidant properties.

INDEX

ACKNOWLEDGMENTS

This book is dedicated to the Clean & Delicious family—a community that continues to encourage and inspire me each day. Thank you!

A FEW MORE THANK-YOUS!

Beng: *Clean & Delicious* would not exist without you. Thank you for believing in me before I learned how to believe in myself.

Katie: My mini me and partner in crime—thank you for always sharing your ideas and insights. You are my teenage sage; wiser then your years and my greatest teacher.

Jachs: My #1 taste tester and family fun-maker! Thank you for shining your beautiful, bright light in all directions at all times.

Laur-Laur: My oldest friend, recipe-testing parter, and go-to girl. Thank you for for always being in the room when I need you.

Helene: You always know how to capture the lighting in the most perfect way. I'm grateful that we were able to shoot this cover together. Thank you for always offering the most thoughtful feedback, ongoing encouragement, and making me the yummiest oat milk lattes.

Julie: Thank you for the longest walks and cookbook talks, and for letting me think it all through out loud. I'm grateful for your positive perspective and unconditional encouragement.

Rikki: Thank you for helping me capture the most beautiful images of my C&D dishes.

Leslie: Thank you for being most fun and easygoing food stylist ever. Thank you for bringing these dishes to life.

Brook and Molly: I had no idea what I was getting into when I started this cookbook. I could not have done this without your patience, guidance, and encouragement. Thank you!